ISAIAH: GOOD NEWS FOR THE WAYWARD AND WANDERING

Jonathan Gibson

STUDY GUIDE WITH LEADER'S NOTES

New
Growth
Press

newgrowthpress.com

New Growth Press, Greensboro, NC 27401
newgrowthpress.com
Copyright © 2022 by Jonathan Gibson

Cover Design: Faceout Books, faceoutstudio.com
Interior Design and Typesetting: Gretchen Logterman
Exercises and Application Questions: Jack Klumpenhower

ISBN 978-1-64507-216-4 (Print
ISBN 978-1-64507-217-1 (eBook)

Printed in the United States of America

29 28 27 26 25 24 23 22   1 2 3 4 5

For my brother Alastair

CONTENTS

ISAIAH'S WORLD

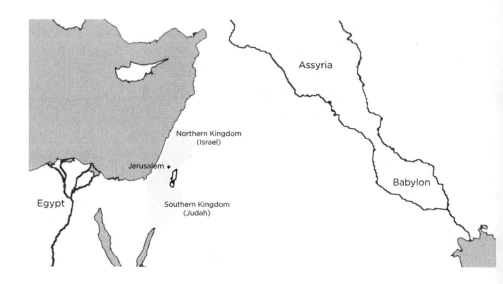

THE NORTHERN KINGDOM

- Called Israel, or sometimes Ephraim after its most notable tribe

- Steeped in idol worship since separating from the Southern Kingdom two centuries before

- Fell to Assyria in 722 BC as judgment for its unfaithfulness; people deported or otherwise assimilated into surrounding cultures

THE SOUTHERN KINGDOM

- Called Judah after its most notable tribe, or sometimes Jerusalem after its capital city
- Original and primary audience of Isaiah's message
- More faithful to God than the Northern Kingdom, but had periods of unchecked sin and idolatry deserving judgment
- Invaded by Assyria in 701 BC, but temporarily spared by God's intervention under the reign of the godly King Hezekiah
- Fell to Babyon in 587 BC; people exiled until a remnant returned seventy years later following an edict by Cyrus, king of Persia

INTRODUCTION

At the book of Isaiah's turning point in chapter 40, where the downbeat of judgment fades and the upbeat of salvation increases, the prophet pictures a massive highway construction project. The road will be God's highway as he comes to rescue his wayward and wandering people. When he travels on it, "the glory of the LORD shall be revealed, and all flesh shall see it together." That's what you are about to see through this study. You will join with others in looking at God's glory revealed in the salvation of his people.

The Hebrew word for glory, *kabod*, conveys a sense of heaviness—a dense and real-as-can-be treasure. When Moses was on Mount Sinai and asked to see God's glory, God said that he would let all his *goodness* pass by. This is what the Lord's glory in Isaiah reveals. It is God's good character, more real and lasting and beautiful than any other prize we might pursue. As you study Isaiah, expect to discover truths about God's goodness—his justice to punish sin and his mercy to forgive sin—that are far more precious than you may have realized.

This glory of God is seen most fully in Jesus Christ. All four gospels take Isaiah's highway picture and apply it to the coming of Jesus, about whom Isaiah has much to say. So, like the other small-group resources in this series, this study will repeatedly point you to the Savior who revealed God's glory by taking our punishment for sin and showering us with mercy. Your discovery of God's glory will be your encounter with God himself.

HOW TO USE THIS STUDY

This study guide is designed to help you learn from Isaiah within a small group. It assumes many of the longings, fears, and doubts that are found in Isaiah are also present in your group. Studying with others will help you see these and serve to encourage each other. With this in mind, try to make the group a place where participants can be open about sins, frustrations, and the hard parts of life. The book of Isaiah itself describes the prophet's original audience as dull and slow to believe the extraordinary message he brought to them, so don't expect every participant to be equally quick to understand or to share personal struggles. Be patient with each other, and allow God's Word to work in his good timing.

Each participant should have one of these study guides in order to join in reading and be able to work through the exercises during that part of the study. The study leader should read through both the lesson and the leader's notes in the back of this book before each lesson begins. No other preparation or homework is required.

Since Isaiah is a lengthy book, only selected portions of the book are covered. On your own, you may want to add to this study by reading through the parts of Isaiah that the study skips. The end of each lesson will tell you what chapters to read in Isaiah before the next lesson if you wish to do so, but you'll be able to participate in the next lesson whether you do the added reading or not.

There are ten lessons in this study guide. Each lesson will take about an hour to complete, perhaps a bit more if your group is large, and will include these elements:

BIG IDEA. This is a summary of the main point of the lesson.

BIBLE CONVERSATION. You will read a passage from Isaiah and discuss it. As the heading suggests, the Bible conversation questions are intended to spark a conversation rather than generate correct answers. The leader's notes at the back of this book provide some insights, but don't just turn there for the "right answer." At times you may want to see what the notes say, but always try to discover the answer for yourself first by thinking about the Bible passage.

ARTICLE. This is the main teaching section of the lesson, written by the book's author.

DISCUSSION. The discussion questions following the article will help you apply the teaching to your life.

EXERCISE. The exercise is a section you will complete on your own during group time. You can write in the book if that helps you. You will then share some of what you learned with the group. If the group is large, it may help to split up to share the results of the exercise and to pray, so that everyone has a better opportunity to participate.

WRAP-UP AND PRAYER. Prayer is a critical part of the lesson because your spiritual growth will happen through God's work in you, not by your self-effort. You will be asking him to do that good work.

Isaiah's message about God's glory specializes in being timeless. As you will see, Isaiah speaks across generations to address people living in a mix of eras and situations, and he peers forward several centuries to describe Jesus with uncanny precision. Be ready for him also to speak God's word to you, whatever your struggles and wherever you live today.

1

REDEEMED BY JUSTICE

BIG IDEA

In Isaiah, we see the gospel story of how God saves his people, through judgment, for the transformation of the world.[1]

BIBLE CONVERSATION *20 MINUTES*

God called Isaiah to be a prophet beginning in about 740 BC. Isaiah's ministry to God's people in and around Jerusalem spanned the next fifty to sixty years, including the reigns of four different kings (Uzziah, Jotham, Ahaz, and Hezekiah). These were stormy, restless years.

<u>Before Isaiah</u>: God's people had already split into two kingdoms. The Northern Kingdom of Israel was unfaithful, soaking in idolatry. The Southern Kingdom of Judah, centered in Jerusalem, was outwardly more faithful. Those people largely maintained the temple worship of God, but also were prone to false-god worship, unjust behavior in daily life, and failure to trust God in times of trouble. Isaiah addresses the Southern Kingdom.

<u>During Isaiah's ministry</u>: God's people faced serious threats of invasion and conquest from regional superpowers. As judgment

for its unrepentant sin, God allowed the Northern Kingdom to be wiped out by Assyria. Assyria also invaded the Southern Kingdom, but God saved Jerusalem under repentant King Hezekiah. Still, judgment for sin was looming and a new superpower, Babylon, was rising.

After Isaiah: Babylon conquered Jerusalem and took its people into exile in 587 BC, but a remnant survived and returned seventy years later to restore the city and reinstate godly worship. About 500 years after that, Jesus came and the gospel message of salvation in him went out to the whole world. Isaiah foresaw all these events and has much to say about them.

But Isaiah's awareness is even broader. All he says takes place against a larger backdrop that spans creation to new creation—the world's beginning to its end. With this in mind, have a few readers take turns reading **Isaiah 1:1–2:5** aloud. Then discuss the questions below as a group:

In this passage, what does God see in his people that he finds wrong? What have you seen that's similar in God's people today?

Verse 18 contains a well-loved phrase about God offering to make our sins white as snow. What else is offered or promised in this part of Isaiah that you find encouraging? Explain.

* * *

Now read the following article from this study's author. Take turns reading it aloud, switching readers at each paragraph break. When you finish reading, discuss the questions at the end of the article.

1

A TALE OF ONE CITY

5 MINUTES

The beginning of Isaiah is like the whole book in miniature. On its surface, the book is a tale of one city, Jerusalem. The first half is about Jerusalem in her rebellious stage, and the second half is about Jerusalem in her redeemed stage. But the people of Jerusalem are a picture of all God's people. And what transforms the city is the gospel—the good news of how God saves his people, through judgment, for the transformation of the world. This means Isaiah is also about how God saves *us*, and about how he will one day transform the whole world.

Here in the opening section, Isaiah introduces us to six aspects of his gospel message. He does so using several pictures, which I will point out as we go. Together, they form a miniature of what the whole book of Isaiah is about: *the gospel story of how God saves his people, through judgment, for the transformation of the world.*

Gospel truth #1: The problem of our sin. The first picture Isaiah gives us is of a Father with rebellious children. This is one of the greatest heartaches for any parent, isn't it? The LORD (it's his personal, covenant name when the Bible prints it in small capital letters) has been intimately involved in his people's upbringing.

Yet, their response is to tell him to get out of their lives: "They have despised the Holy One of Israel" (1:4).

Notice that sin is first of all a problem between us and God. We spurn the God who made us, loves us, and cares for us. Notice also that sin makes us permanently sick; it becomes a lingering wound that cannot be "softened with oil" (v. 6). This picture shows that when we sin, it's not so easy to stop. We become stubborn. We would rather stay sick than ask for healing. We can't save ourselves; God has to step in.

Gospel truth #2: The futility of our religious show. When we fall into sin, we mustn't think our religious offerings and festivals and prayers will save us. God says, "I will not listen; your hands are full of blood" (v. 15). Religiously keeping Sunday while morally sleeping Monday through Saturday is hypocrisy. Read the list in verse 17 and ask yourself if this is at the forefront of your Christian life: ceasing from evil, doing good, seeking justice, correcting oppression, helping the helpless and needy.

Gospel truth #3: The call to repent. When God confronts us with our sin and exposes the futility of our religious show, he then calls us to turn from our rebellious ways and walk in his righteous ways. It's the picture of having a bath: "Wash yourselves; make yourselves clean" (v. 16). The picture of the bath also conveys the need for continual cleansing. Salvation is only for people who have turned from their sin and who *continue* to turn from their sin when confronted with it.

Gospel truth #4: The choice of forgiveness or punishment. When we lived in Cambridge, we had blackberries in our garden, and our young son Ben was good at picking them from the bramble bushes. Unfortunately, he was also good at getting blackberry juice on his clothes. So what did we do? We got out the stain remover. That's the next picture here. The gospel comes to us with a picture of the world's best stain remover for sin. God turns our blood-red stains of sin to snow-white purity. He offers complete forgiveness in the form of cleansing. The gospel call to repent is a choice between forgiveness or punishment, restoration or destruction, cleansing or defilement.

But there's a tension here. Remember how God is the Holy One of Israel. How can a holy God remain just and punish sin, and at the same time forgive the same sin? That's the dilemma Isaiah has created, and his answer is surprising: *through a judgment that saves*.

Gospel truth #5: The promise of salvation through judgment. Here's the big surprise: God's judgment on Jerusalem is pictured as a fiery furnace from which good metal emerges. "I will turn my hand against you and will smelt away your dross. . . . Afterward you shall be called the city of righteousness, the faithful city" (vv. 25–26). The judgment will not annihilate God's people; it will purify them. Yes, they will need to go through the judgment into exile in Babylon, but there will be survivors—a new city, transformed from faithless to faithful.

Why can this change occur? Because what happens to Jerusalem here also ends up happening to a person in Jerusalem. It happens to Jesus Christ, the representative of his people. On the cross, he is the Suffering Servant who experiences God's judgment. Out of the grave, he is the sole (remnant) survivor who experiences God's salvation. This is how the Holy One of Israel offers to turn our sins from crimson red to snowy white. Jesus receives our punishment in our place, and by faith we receive his righteousness. This is why "Zion shall be redeemed by justice, and those in her who repent, by righteousness" (v. 27). Justice falls on Jesus, and so righteousness rests on us.

Gospel truth #6: The transformation of the world. The mountain in chapter 2 so surpasses other mountains that it obviously is no longer the earthly Jerusalem but that city's fulfillment—the heavenly Jerusalem where Jesus is King. As the word about Jesus goes out to the nations (v. 3), people hear the good news and repent and are magnetically drawn into this kingdom. The ultimate result is universal peace, seen in a beautiful picture of swords and spears turned into ploughshares and pruning hooks. The instruments that execute a war become instruments that reap a harvest.

So let us live now with the end in mind. Let us repent of our sin that has made us sick. Let us accept the offer of forgiveness. Let us do good and seek justice, because the world is heading for universal peace and the question is whether or not we will be a part of that—part of the gospel story of God saving his people, through judgment, for the transformation of the world.

DISCUSSION *10 MINUTES*

Which of these gospel pictures is personally meaningful to you, and why?

- Rebellious child
- Lingering wound
- Having a bath
- Stain remover
- Furnace that purifies
- Instruments of war becoming instruments of harvest

What response do you have to the truth that salvation comes only *through judgment* received by Jesus when he died on the cross?

Lesson

EXERCISE

REPENTANCE AND FAITH

20 MINUTES

As he does in Isaiah 1, God constantly calls his people to repent of sin and have faith in him. These two habits mark the internal life of a believer. They empower and direct our external behavior.

Whether or not you are a believer in Jesus, God is calling you in Isaiah 1 to repent and have faith. Both halves of Isaiah mention not only God's people but also the surrounding nations. This makes the book's message not just for those who are already part of God's family but also for anyone interested in joining. Whether you already believe or are still exploring Christianity, looking closely at the Christian lifestyle of repentance and faith will help you.

For this exercise, begin by working on your own. First learn what it means to repent and have faith by reading the descriptions below, which are drawn from this lesson's article and our passage in Isaiah. Then you'll answer some questions about yourself. When the group is ready, you'll have a chance to share some of your responses.

REPENTANCE: I see and admit, and deeply feel, my sin problem.

1. With sadness, I admit that I get rebellious toward my Creator and selfish toward others.

2. In remorse, I admit that my sin is not just a few mistakes I make, but a self-seeking heart that wishes to have its own way.

3. In distress, I admit that my sin is a lingering sickness: my natural bent is to stubbornly return to sin again and again, and to resist healing.

REPENTANCE: I come to grips with the futility of my own efforts.

4. I give up the "I've got this" delusion that I can perform well enough to convince God to accept me.

5. I have true sorrow over the times I've been outwardly religious while remaining inwardly cold toward God.

6. I reorient my life to truly love what is good and just and merciful, and to no longer be about a show I put on for God, others, or my conscience.

REPENTANCE: I heed the call to come and be clean.

7. I learn to hate my rebellion and selfishness, and to love being clean.

8. I have an inward change of purpose, turning away from sin and toward godliness.

9. I have an inward change of dependency, turning away from self-reliance and toward Christ-reliance.

FAITH: I agree to take Jesus as my Savior.

> 10. I see that God's offer to turn sin "white as snow" is for me, and I embrace it with gladness.

> 11. I trust Jesus alone to be my stain remover and purifier, not relying on my own sincerity or level of good behavior.

> 12. Jesus becomes all-important to me—my only place of true safety and the person to whom I offer total surrender.

FAITH: I believe and trust Jesus for forgiveness.

> 13. I believe and trust that Jesus took the punishment I deserve, in my place, when he died for me on the cross, and in return gives me his perfect record of righteousness.

> 14. I believe and trust that Jesus is the Son of God, a sacrifice of infinite value that fully and forever pays for even my deepest, repeated sins.

> 15. I believe and trust that Jesus has satisfied God's judgment against me so that now I enjoy God's fatherly favor and care, not constant disapproval.

FAITH: I believe and trust Jesus for renewal.

> 16. I am encouraged by the assurance that, in Christ, my future is bright rather than bleak.

> 17. I believe and trust that God is making me righteous and faithful like Jesus, and I joyfully answer God's call to cooperate with his work in me.

> 18. I believe and trust that Jesus will return to judge the world, raise my body from the dead, end evil and sadness, gather his people from the nations, and live forever with me in a city of peace.

Now pick the question set below that best fits you. Select an item or two from the descriptions of repentance and faith to answer each question. You might mark your responses or write down the numbers if that helps you keep track of your answers.

If you are *not* yet a believer in Jesus, or are not sure . . .

Which of the descriptions above especially feel like something you don't yet wish to do, or can't do?

Which do you most find appealing about the Christian life?

Which do you think most stand in the way of you believing in Jesus?

Which ones most draw you toward Jesus?

If you *are* a believer in Jesus . . .

Which of the descriptions above are particularly difficult for you?

Which come to mind as being something you've done recently?

Which would you especially like to see become a bigger part of your life?

Which ones most draw you closer to Jesus?

When the group is ready, share some of your responses and explain why you chose them.

WRAP-UP AND PRAYER *10 MINUTES*

Prayer is a main way we put our faith into practice, so do that now as a part of your group prayer time. Repentance and faith are gifts from God that he works in us, so ask him to give you hearts that are repentant and faithful. Pray that he would use your time together in Isaiah to do this.

MORE READING: If you wish to read through all of Isaiah as part of this study, read Isaiah 2:6–5:30 before the next lesson, which will be on chapter 6.

2

HOLY, HOLY, HOLY

BIG IDEA

Amid life's uncertainties, we need to see our holy God on his throne—revealing our sin, restoring our status, and sending us on his mission.

BIBLE CONVERSATION *20 MINUTES*

Isaiah 6 begins by mentioning the death of King Uzziah, the first of the four kings who reigned in Jerusalem while Isaiah was a prophet. Uzziah was both a godly king and a long-serving one (fifty-two years on the throne!) with an impressive record of making his nation secure, providing God's people with both political and religious stability.* Isaiah likely began his ministry as a court prophet to Uzziah. Isaiah's report of the vision he saw in the year of Uzziah's death includes a few terms we need to understand:

Holy comes from the verb *to set apart* and can describe objects or people kept pure for God. Here it is used in a bigger way to praise God himself. It means all the majestic "otherness" of God that sets God above every created thing. It's the hard-to-even-fathom distinctness of God that makes God *God*.

---

* See 2 Chronicles 26:1–15.

Glory is also hard to comprehend. The Hebrew word literally means "weighty." It is the splendid richness of everything good about God that is revealed when God shows himself or his handiwork, and the honor he receives for it.

Seraphim are fiery creatures of heaven, probably angels of some sort.

Now have someone read all of **Isaiah 6** aloud, or have a few readers take turns. Then discuss the questions below:

What do the details in this passage suggest about God, and how does this differ from popular ideas of what God is like?

How does Isaiah's interaction with God differ from popular ideas of what it would be like to meet God?

What might you like, or dislike, about being given the sort of mission Isaiah receives from God? Explain.

****

Next, take turns reading the article aloud, switching readers at each paragraph break. After reading the article, discuss the questions that follow.

WHEN OUR WORLD FALLS APART

5 MINUTES

In countries with monarchies, there is a saying when the king or queen dies: "The king is dead, long live the king." It's a saying that is meant to stop uncertainty, stave off instability, and solve the crisis over who's in charge. The king is dead, but long live the new king. And that's what Isaiah sees at the start of chapter 6, only it's not Uzziah's son Jotham on his throne in the palace. It's the Lord on his throne in heaven. The king is dead, long live *the* King.

When our world is in crisis, we need to see that God is seated on his throne. When life throws unsettling things at us—tragic family news, a shocking medical diagnosis, or whatever—we are quickly reminded that we are not in control. We are not the king or queen of our own lives. That king is dead. But long live the King. The Lord is on his throne. He is not the least bit anxious about how things will play out, because he is holy. He is wholly other than we are. He is God and we are not.

God's holy otherness is so above all things that even the seraphim, who don't have any taint of sin on them, can't look at him and instead cover their eyes. They can't approach him and instead cover their feet. What is left for them to do? They sing, repeating words from the far fringes of language, the only words we have to express what is inexpressible: "Holy, holy, holy is the LORD of hosts; the whole earth is full of his glory!"

Isaiah saw God's holy transcendence and holy purity. This is what we too need to see when "the king is dead"—when as a nation we experience turmoil, or when a crisis flies into our personal lives. We need to hear the angels singing that God is holy, because only the gravity of who God is can provide rock-solid certainty and stability in times of turbulence. As with Isaiah, when our world falls apart, here are three things we need.

First, we need to see ourselves in our sinfulness. For Isaiah, the temple's shaking thresholds and blinding smoke have already made it obvious he cannot approach God. But unlike the seraphim, he can't sing either, because he is a man of unclean lips. He can only blurt out, "Woe is me! For I am lost!"

Who uses a word like *woe* anymore? Someone who's in the presence of the thrice holy God, that's who! Isaiah realizes that he is doomed. The prophet, who'd had it all together in the royal courts of the great King Uzziah, now comes apart—broken in pieces like Humpty Dumpty. Why? Because his eyes have seen the true King. Having experienced God's *wow*, he knows his own *woe*.

A lot of people intellectually see their sin but never change because they never *feel* their sin in light of the Lord of hosts who is holy, holy, holy. Our shame about our sin should affect our psychological disposition. Otherwise, it falls short of godly sorrow—and that's what we need. In moments of uncertainty and instability, we need to come to the end of ourselves. But then . . .

Second, we need to experience the Lord's restoration. Only once we've come undone will we welcome the good news that our King doesn't leave us like Humpty Dumpty but puts us back together again. Notice how passive Isaiah is as the angel brings a coal and touches it to his lips. This is *God's* work, applied to the most sensitive part of the body and the very place Isaiah feels his sin the most. God restores his whole person by dealing first with his core problem of sin and guilt.

Notice how it comes about: by a King high and lifted up who provides atonement from an altar of sacrifice. This vision is fulfilled in Jesus, who left his heavenly throne to be lifted up on an altar of sacrifice—the cross. And it all comes from God's holiness. The same holiness that exposes our sin atones for our sin. At the cross, God punishes sin because he is *holy righteous* and *holy just,* and he also forgives sin because he is *holy gracious* and *holy merciful.* The cross is where we receive God's forgiving touch on our lives—at the very place where we most need it.

Third, we need to give ourselves to the Lord's mission. When we receive his forgiving touch, God prepares us for service. This is what happened to Isaiah. But look at his calling: it's a ministry of hardening that leads to judgment. This is another preview of Jesus, who in Mark 4 quoted Isaiah to explain that he taught in parables so people would *not* understand and *not* repent—to harden their hearts.

Yes, Jesus preached to harden hearts, but only as a means to a greater end. The hard hearts of the people and their religious leaders eventually led to his crucifixion, and out of that moment of judgment came salvation. The two-beat rhythm of biblical history is judgment-salvation. Jesus's death on the cross was the climactic judgment-salvation event in biblical history, with salvation as the final beat.

This is why being part of God's mission is well worth our time and commitment. It is because, amid all our world's instabilities and our many personal uncertainties, and despite the hard hearts and heavy blows we often encounter, God is saving a people for himself. For each of us, our involvement in the proclamation of this gospel will be different. Some will go to the nations. Others will stay and pray and give and serve in their church. But we should all be involved in God's mission. Because if we've seen the Lord on his throne in his holiness, felt our sinfulness, and experienced his restoration, how else should we spend our lives?

DISCUSSION *10 MINUTES*

How much do you *feel* your sin and the good news of restoration, or do you just acknowledge it intellectually? Share examples if you can.

How has feeling your sin and restoration changed the way you live your life?

LONG LIVE KING JESUS

20 MINUTES

You might wish you too could have a life-changing vision like Isaiah did. Well, according to the Gospel of John, you can and you do! John 1:14 tells us that because Jesus has come to us, "we have seen [God's] glory, glory as of the only Son from the Father, full of grace and truth." And John 12:41 says that it was *Jesus's* glory Isaiah saw and spoke of—a vision of the Son of God before he came to earth as a man. According to the apostle Paul, you see God's glory "in the face of Jesus Christ" (2 Corinthians 4:6). And you see it with details Isaiah never knew—not just the glory of Jesus's throne, but also the glories of his humble birth, his compassion, his cross, his resurrection, his prayers for you, and much more.

On your own, read through the items below. Each begins with a way some "king" in your life might be dead—a troubling situation that exposes your frailty. That's followed by a look at the glory of King Jesus, who lives. Pick a few items (not all of them) that fit you. Make those items personal by adding an explanation of how your king is dead and a thought about how seeing Jesus might encourage you to serve God. Later, you'll have a chance to share some of your responses.

The king is dead. I feel <u>threatened by upheaval</u> in the world, my nation, or my community, or I am worried about troubling developments in my work, my family, or my church.

Explain:

Long live King Jesus. No other powers can stand against Jesus, who is on my side and is having his way even when he lets evil seem to win for the moment. "He raised [Christ] from the dead and seated him at his right hand in the heavenly places, far above all rule and authority and power and dominion, and above every name that is named" (Ephesians 1:20–21).

Freed from insecurity, I might serve God's mission by:

The king is dead. A recent <u>death</u>, or an impending one (perhaps my own!), has made me sad or fearful about the fragility of life.

Explain:

Long live King Jesus. Jesus is in charge of death and, even more, he is the Lord of resurrection who will raise me from the grave. "He laid his right hand on me, saying, 'Fear not, I am the first and the last, and the living one. I died, and behold I am alive forevermore, and I have the keys of Death and Hades'" (Revelation 1:17–18).

Freed from the fear of death, I might serve God's mission by:

The king is dead. A health, financial, or other personal crisis is hounding me.

Explain:

Long live King Jesus. Jesus showed tireless compassion while on earth. He will never leave my side, and will only let me suffer what is good for me. "Jesus went throughout all the cities and villages . . . healing every disease and every affliction. When he saw the crowds, he had compassion for them, because they were harassed and helpless" (Matthew 9:35–36).

Freed from the fear of a crisis, I might serve God's mission by:

The king is dead. I am undone by my sin, which feels like it condemns me and leaves me with a nagging fear that God may be planning to take out his judgment on me.

Explain:

Long live King Jesus. The unapproachable King in Isaiah's vision is the *same person* who left his throne in heaven and became the most approachable man ever—even dying for my sin. He says, "Whoever comes to me I will never cast out. For I have come down from heaven" (John 6:37–38).

Freed from the fear of judgment, I might serve God's mission by:

The king is dead. My <u>self-effort to please God</u> has failed, leaving me only with a sense that God is usually annoyed, disappointed, or impatient with me for not obeying him better.

Explain:

Long live King Jesus. One reason Jesus lives forever is to always intercede for me with God, and to continually, gently help me. "We do not have a high priest who is unable to sympathize with our weaknesses, but one who in every respect has been tempted as we are, yet without sin. Let us then with confidence draw near to the throne of grace, that we may receive mercy and find grace to help in time of need" (Hebrews 4:15–16).

Freed from the <u>burden of self-effort</u>, I might serve God's mission by:

prayer

√ **The king is dead.** In a world where people reject Jesus, I feel <u>powerless to make any progress</u> or to have an impact for Christ's kingdom.

Explain:

Long live King Jesus. Jesus encourages me not to grow weary, promising that "in due season we will reap" (Galatians 6:9). He taught that his kingdom surely is life-giving like a mustard seed: "It is the smallest of all seeds, but when it has grown it is larger than all the garden plants and becomes a tree, so that the birds of the air come and make nests in its branches" (Matthew 13:32).

Freed from <u>disappointment's st</u>ing, I might serve God's mission by:

When the group is ready, share some of your responses. Which of Jesus's glories encourage you to serve God, and how?

WRAP-UP AND PRAYER *10 MINUTES*

Consider focusing your prayer time around the three experiences Isaiah had during his vision: confess your sin, thank God for the restoration he gives, and pray for missions (either your own involvement or the work of others).

Also, before you leave Isaiah 6, look again at its closing words. After much judgment, what does God leave standing? A holy seed. A stump. Well, stumps can grow new shoots—a remnant, a few survivors. And indeed, in our next lesson it will turn out to be *one* survivor, one holy seed who changes everything.

MORE READING: If you are reading through all of Isaiah, read chapters 7 through 10 before the next lesson, which will be on chapter 11.

Elisabeth Cherney
Phillips

3

A SHOOT FROM THE STUMP OF JESSE

BIG IDEA

In our desire for a good life and a better world, Jesus gives us a sure hope—with rightness and results no other leader can match.

BIBLE CONVERSATION *20 MINUTES*

At the end of Isaiah 6, we saw a message of judgment against God's people in Jerusalem. It mentioned a desolate land, with a single stump the only remaining sign of hope. The chapters that follow tell how Assyria will be like an axe of judgment in God's hand (indeed, Assyria scorched the land and nearly took Jerusalem before God ended the onslaught). But chapter 10 ends with God judging Assyria too: the axe itself gets chopped down by God and its own forests fall. It turns out God was simply using Assyria for a little while as part of a greater purpose. There's a wider judgment *everyone* faces, seen in how there are now remnant stumps of judgment everywhere.

This brings us to Isaiah 11, where new life grows from just one stump called "the stump of Jesse." Jesse was the father of King David, so the prophecy that follows is about a king over God's people, like David was. But why not call it "the stump of *David*"? Perhaps because this king will not just be in the line of David but will be someone grander—a new and better David, with whom God will begin a new dynasty.

This chapter also mentions Judah and Ephraim, rival tribes of God's people, and many surrounding nations that gave them trouble. Judah is the southern nation centered in Jerusalem. Ephraim represents the unfaithful, northern nation which Assyria defeated and scattered two decades before the attack on Jerusalem.

Have a volunteer read all of **Isaiah 11** aloud, or have a few readers take turns. Then discuss the questions below:

Think about leaders in your life. What would you appreciate about having the kind of leader described in verses 2–5?

How do you feel when you try to imagine the coming world as it is described in verses 6–9? Explain.

The last half of the passage borrows imagery from the exodus that occurred centuries earlier, when God rescued his people from slavery in Egypt. What do you find even more exciting about the new exodus God has planned, described here?

****

Now read this lesson's article aloud, taking turns by paragraph. When you finish, discuss the questions at the end of the article.

Lesson

ARTICLE

EDEN-TOPIA

5 MINUTES

By now, you should be settling into the two-beat rhythm of Isaiah: Judgment. Salvation. But that's not all there is. Remember that we've summarized Isaiah's message as *the gospel story of how God saves his people, through judgment, **for the transformation of the world***. This transformation is where we arrive in Isaiah 11. It's a vision of a world we might be tempted to label *utopia*—a place so perfect it must be a fantasy.

All political and world leaders promise their people a better place. But politicians who make great promises make great liars, because they never deliver on their fantasies. Here in Isaiah we have a different kind of king, "a shoot from the stump of Jesse," who delivers on everything he promises. What makes this coming king better? There are four things:

First, notice the king's Spirit. Other leaders lack wisdom and courage to make the right decisions. They fear what people think. They have feet of clay. They cannot do great things for God because they do not have the Spirit of God.

But look how dependent on the Spirit this king will be. The Spirit will give him wisdom and understanding to make good judgments.

The Spirit will give him counsel and might to be strategic and strong in battle. And the Spirit will give him knowledge and fear of the Lord—a stark contrast to King Ahaz who feared enemy invaders and groveled before Assyria earlier in Isaiah. The coming king will not care what others think, only what God thinks. He will seek God's approval in all he does.

Second, notice the king's manner. Even the most unwavering world leaders negotiate, compromise, give favors, and spin stories to further their agendas. But the coming king will have an unshakeable commitment to what is right and true. Righteousness and faithfulness will define his character, just as they adorn God's character.

And there's something more that makes this king God-like. The best of human leaders can't provide absolute justice because they don't have absolute knowledge. But the coming king won't judge by what he sees or hears; he knows evidence that *can't* be seen and heard. He'll judge by absolute knowledge.

Third, notice the king's reign. Rather than a fantasy utopia, we might describe the resulting kingdom as Eden-topia. It's a paradise place, with echoes of the garden of Eden. Old hostilities are reconciled, as predator and prey live together. Old natures are transformed, as lions eat straw. And the old curse is eliminated.[2] Back in Genesis 3:15, God set in motion the ages-old conflict between us and the serpent, and he promised an offspring of the woman who would crush the serpent's head. The picture here is of the end of that conflict: "The nursing child shall play over the hole of the cobra" (v. 8).

The coming king's reign will completely remove all danger and injury and death. The devil will threaten no more, and universal peace will reign. The whole earth "shall be full of the knowledge of the LORD as the waters cover the sea" (v. 9). That's 100 percent saturation. It's a beautiful picture of the certainty and scale of the world's transformation under this king's reign. He will restore Eden and raise it to a state Adam never saw, and will make it permanent and irreversible.

Finally, notice the king's exodus. Starting in verse 10, Isaiah suddenly changes his imagery. He begins by calling the coming king "the root of Jesse." A shoot and a root are not the same thing. It turns out that the king who is a shoot from the stump of Jesse is also Jesse's root—that is, he will be a descendant of Jesse and yet also the origin of Jesse.

Then Isaiah describes the king as a signal to the nations, like a banner flying high for an international meeting point. The king will draw all God's people to himself. Once again, they will have unity. Once again, they will come out of slavery, and the king himself will be their exodus.

Do you see it? The transformation of the world will come about by a king who has the Spirit of God rest upon him, whose manner will be righteous and faithful, whose reign will cast out the devil and bring Eden-topia, and who will be a rescuer for his people. And so we're left asking ourselves: Just who is this king? No mere earthly leader fits. He can be none other than *the* King, Jesus Christ.

In John 12:31–32, a few days before he was lifted up on the cross, Jesus announced, "Now is the judgment of the world; now will the ruler of this world be cast out. And I, when I am lifted up from the earth, will draw all people to myself." Crucified, he saves his people from slavery to sin, by undergoing judgment. Risen from the dead and ascended to heaven, he finds a glorious resting place at his Father's right hand and from there gathers the nations to himself.

Still today, the gospel goes to the nations and people are drawn to the banner of this King. Yes, every other leader promises a better place, a good place. But it's more fantasy than reality—utopia. Only Jesus Christ can promise (and deliver) a perfect place; only he can restore and consummate what the original creation was meant to be—Eden-topia. Remember his words to the dying thief on the cross? "Today you will be with me in *paradise*."

DISCUSSION *10 MINUTES*

Which side of Jesus, his impeccable character or his unheard-of results, do people seem to find hardest to believe?

When you first came to Jesus, what was it that drew you to him? Or what do you find most compelling as you consider Jesus today?

EXERCISE

YOUR SOURCE OF HOPE

20 MINUTES

We all hope for a good life and a better world. We trust leaders, causes, our personal achievements, and more. Many of these might be good things, but they can become *the* thing you trust for a better life, or a better world, instead of putting your hope in Jesus.

For this exercise, you'll work on your own to complete several sentences. First, you'll identify things you tend to trust other than Jesus. Complete the sentence if you can think of a response that's true of you, or skip it if you can't. Then use Isaiah 11 to complete three more sentences with ways Jesus is more worthy of your trust. Be prepared to share some of your results after you finish.

Leader. Complete the sentence by naming a political/government leader, a church leader or popular preacher/teacher, a leader in your family, or some other leader who influences how you see the world—so that you might be putting more hope in that leader than you should.

To make the world better, I trust the values, influence, and power of _Church – conservative values_

_____.

Cause. Complete the sentence by adding a social action, a political faction, a religious movement/camp or effort to protect/improve the church, or some other cause in which you hope.

Things would head in the right direction if we could advance the cause of _Republican party, Reformed faith_

_____.

Achievement. Complete the sentence with a career or some kind of work, a desire for your family, an educational goal, a spiritual attainment, an athletic/artistic accomplishment, a social status, or some other achievement in which you hope.

I figure I ought to have a good life if I can be successful at _____ _making money / obtaining financial security_

_____.

Approval. Complete the sentence with an area where you seek recognition for your religious devotion, your church involvement, the kind of family you've built, your career, your appearance, your social/financial standing, the impact you make in the world, or some other approval you cherish.

I feel good about my life when others recognize me for _____ _helping them_

_____.

Viewpoint. Complete the sentence by mentioning how things should be in politics, government, the church, your family, your workplace, or something else you are convinced people need to understand.

Everything would be better if people would just think rightly about _Christ, less govt involvement_

_____.

Stability. Complete the sentence by noting some financial security, health assurance, family/relationship status, physical security or preparedness, emotional stability, home establishment, or some other assurance in your life.

I think life will be all right, and I feel secure, when I have stability in my _nothing is breaking - car/house_

_____.

Now that you've identified some places you put your hope, consider how Jesus is better. What does he deliver that's bigger than what your other hopes offer? How is he surer and more lasting? Look back through Isaiah 11. Find some phrases that remind you how Jesus is even more trustworthy and reliable than the things you noted above. Use those phrases from Isaiah 11 to complete the sentences below.

Jesus is better because he _is better than the church/govt._

_____.

Jesus is better because he _____

_____.

Jesus is better because he _____

_____.

When the group is ready, share some of your responses. Where do you put your hope, and how is Jesus better?

How does the source of your hope affect your daily behavior?

anxiety + fixated + distraction

How might your excitement for God's mission in the world change if you more fully believed that Jesus offers a better hope?

WRAP-UP AND PRAYER *10 MINUTES*

The Bible expects us to pray for Jesus to return and for his coming kingdom to be fully realized: "Come, Lord Jesus!" (Revelation 22:20). So, include this in your prayer time together. Also pray that you would be encouraged by Jesus's coming kingdom and would put your hope in him, "that you may stand mature and fully assured in all the will of God" (Colossians 4:12).

MORE READING: If you are reading through all of Isaiah, read chapters 12 through 25 before the next lesson, which will be on chapter 26.

Lesson

4

THE DESIRE OF OUR SOUL

BIG IDEA

In Jesus our salvation is assured, but we must wait for it in a troubled and frustrating world, learning to hope and hide in our Savior.

BIBLE CONVERSATION *20 MINUTES*

Following the vision of Jesus's coming kingdom in chapter 11, the book of Isaiah describes judgment upon the nations that surround and threaten God's people, ending with another celebration of the kingdom to come: "He will swallow up death forever; and the Lord GOD will wipe away tears from all faces" (25:8). Chapter 26 is a song that will be sung when that happy day arrives. The song itself, though, looks back on the days of judgment God's people will go through to get to the days of celebration.

This means that the song teaches us how to *wait for the Lord* as we live under the shadow of his common curse in a fallen world of sin and tears and death: "In the path of your judgments, O LORD, we wait for you" (v. 8). The people in Isaiah's day had to wait for God's deliverance as Assyria invaded their land. A few generations later, they would wait to return to Jerusalem after the judgment of exile in Babylon. Then they would wait centuries for Jesus to be born. And today, we too wait between the pain of this world and the promise of Jesus's return.

Have a few readers take turns reading all of **Isaiah 26** aloud. Then discuss the questions below:

Much of the song contrasts the people of God's "strong city" (v. 1) with those who live in the "lofty city" of the world (v. 5). What spiritual differences between the two peoples do you notice, and where do those differences lead?

Verses 9–10 and verse 16 suggest that hard times, rather than good times, often cause us to seek God. How have these lines in the song been true in your life?

Verses 16–21 describe both utter frustration and amazing hope. How do you react to the song's words, and to the idea that frustration and hope coexist for God's people?

****

Now read this lesson's article aloud, taking turns by paragraph. Then discuss the questions that follow.

ARTICLE

4

WAITING FOR THE LORD

5 MINUTES

There's something about going through a great trial in life. Like a purifying furnace, it burns away the fluff and makes us long for the Lord. In the world, we see this when a disaster happens and people who normally don't think of God suddenly talk about the disaster victims being in their "thoughts and prayers." And as Christians, we too are drawn to God when we walk the paths of his judgments, as verse 8 puts it. God brings brokenness into our lives in this world that is cursed due to sin, and it is meant to make us hunger for him: "My soul yearns for you in the night; my spirit within me earnestly seeks you" (v. 9).

The question is: How long must we wait and yearn? We are only told that the sore providences God sends our way are temporary. The Lord's "hand is lifted up" (v. 11), meaning he is acting for his people even in the midst of painful times. One day, those who have oppressed us will be dead and gone: "They will not live" (v. 14), wiped out without remembrance. There will be no memorial stone to the devil or to death in the heavenly city.

But what do we do when we feel like the curse is not passing, the shadow is never lifting, the pain and problems are not going away? What do we do when life takes a turn for the worst and feels like it'll never get back on track? What do we do when some of us die without seeing any end to our suffering or hardship or trial? In other words, what do we do when we are in *total despair*?

Well, Isaiah gives us a picture of that total despair. In verse 16, he speaks of distress that has laid God's people so low they can only whisper a prayer. And then he shows how distressful this distress can get, how despairing the despair can be, with one of the Bible's most graphic pictures: "We were pregnant, we writhed, but we have given birth to wind" (v. 18).

The people writhed in pain, but there was no end-product. No baby. No new life. Just wind. Wind is a picture of meaninglessness. The time under God's hardships felt fruitless: "We have accomplished no deliverance in the earth" (v. 18). That's how we can feel too, isn't it? When God's hand rests heavy on us, it might feel as if it has served no purpose in our lives.

In recent years, I've known people who have lost so much as they've lived under the shadow of God's common curse: a friend who held her son for just an hour after his birth before he died, another whose life's work was wiped out by an unintentional mistake, a family member whose shares dissolved in a financial downturn. In each case, there was total despair. They couldn't get the son back, couldn't get the work back, couldn't get the shares back. They're all gone, like the wind. And it's hard to see how God had any purpose or brought any progress from it.

What are we to do when life gets that difficult, that depressing? Well, most of Isaiah 26 is our song addressed to God. But notice that in verse 19, God begins to speak to us. Finally, we hear the voice of God, which is just what we need to hear when it feels like there's nothing but despair and death all around us. God gives us two things to do:

First, we are to hope in the Lord. Listen to what God says:

> Your dead shall live; their bodies shall rise.
>> You who dwell in the dust, awake and sing for joy!
> For your dew is a dew of light,
>> and the earth will give birth to the dead.

You see, some of those in Judah who went through the judgment under Assyria and Babylon never came out on the other end. They went into their graves. They died in a foreign land. And so, their judgment felt like the end judgment, more like annihilation than purification.

But then God speaks. His people will not be like the despotic leaders of the lofty city, whose bodies lie dead and will not rise, and who have no remembrance. For the righteous, for those in the strong city of God whose lives ended in seeming pointlessness, there will be resurrection! Awakening. A joyful song. The dew of light, a picture of the morning sun on moistened grass. Resurrection morning is the end for every Christian—not despair or death.

Yes, you might end this life never seeing the fruit of any of your trials, but see what message God himself speaks to you in Isaiah's song. Even in the grave, your body awaits the rising sun—or better, the risen Son. Your Savior did not end his story hanging on a cross or cold in a tomb, and neither will you if you are united to him. Your life will not end in despair on a Friday evening; it will end in joy on a Sunday morning—because that's how things turned out for your Savior.

And second, having hoped in the Lord, God beckons us also to hide in him. God's personal speech continues: "Hide yourselves for a little while until the fury has passed by" (v. 20). The song ends with the Lord coming in judgment to punish those on the earth who have sinned, and to expose all that is wrong. We too need shelter, because we're just as sinful as the next person. This is why our Lord calls us to come to him, and hide in him.

As New Testament Christians, our shelter is found in Jesus Christ and in his life, death, resurrection, and ascension. He is how we wait for the Lord; he is how we hide. We hope in him and hide in him as the final judgment approaches. This is the way God has made us to live in his world, under the shadow of his common curse, amid sin and tears and death: always hoping, always hiding.

DISCUSSION *10 MINUTES*

What frustrations in your life feel like they will never go away? Explain.

How might your life today change if you thought more about your life after death—if your hope of resurrection was greater?

Lesson

EXERCISE

TRUST, LONG, HOPE, AND HIDE

20 MINUTES

The Bible conversation and the article have brought out four ways Isaiah 26 teaches us to respond to Jesus amid distress: trust him (v. 4), long for him (v. 9), hope in him (v. 19), and hide in him (v. 20).

On your own, read the items below and consider how you might wait for the Lord in this fallen, sinful world. Pick some items that are especially meaningful to you for one of the following reasons:

- You've seen evidence of God working them in you.
- They make you feel especially thankful.
- They represent a lifestyle that, by God's work in you, you would like to see become truer of you.

When the group is ready, you'll share some of the items you chose and tell why you find them meaningful.

TRUSTING in Jesus

☐ In every concern I have, my go-to response is to pray. I remember that Jesus is my strong city, always eager to help me. "Casting all your anxieties on him, because he cares for you" (1 Peter 5:7).

☐ I give up being my own lofty city, proud of how I can survive in the world and feeling superior to others. Instead, I let myself look foolish, needy, or weak—relying on Jesus to be strong. "I will boast all the more gladly of my weaknesses, so that the power of Christ may rest upon me" (2 Corinthians 12:9).

☐ Amid all kinds of troubles, I cultivate the perfect peace that comes from a mind anchored in Jesus (v. 3). I soak daily in his words, promises, and saving works. "Let the peace of Christ rule in your hearts, to which indeed you were called in one body. And be thankful. Let the word of Christ dwell in you richly" (Colossians 3:15–16).

LONGING for Jesus

☐ I treasure time spent with Jesus, in prayer and feeding on his Word—privately, with other believers, and in the worshiping assembly of God's people. "Do not work for the food that perishes, but for the food that endures to eternal life, which the Son of Man will give to you" (John 6:27).

☐ Close fellowship with other believers is dear to me. Together, we live close to Jesus. "Be filled with the Spirit, addressing one another in psalms and hymns and spiritual songs, singing and making melody to the Lord with your heart" (Ephesians 5:18–19).

☐ My prayer life is not a burden, but has become burden-lifting. I have learned to find joy and relief in coming near to Jesus. "The Lord is at hand; do not be anxious about anything, but in everything by prayer and supplication with thanksgiving let your requests be made known to God" (Philippians 4:5–6).

HOPING in Jesus

☐ I stop living for worldly comforts and amassing earthly treasures, which are only wind. My hope is set instead on lasting, heavenly riches. "Provide yourselves with moneybags that do not grow old, with a treasure in the heavens that does not fail, where no thief approaches and no moth destroys" (Luke 12:33).

☐ The resurrection of Jesus is a beacon to me. I navigate this world driven by the expectation that I will follow my Savior into death and then into new life. "He has caused us to be born again to a living hope through the resurrection of Jesus Christ from the dead, to an inheritance that is imperishable, undefiled, and unfading, kept in heaven for you" (1 Peter 1:3–4).

☐ Even in great sadness, I have an underlying joy. I am free of the fear of endless death or endless sorrow, knowing that one day even the devil will have no remembrance. "That through death [Christ] might destroy the one who has the power of death, that is, the devil, and deliver all those who through fear of death were subject to lifelong slavery" (Hebrews 2:14–15).

HIDING in Jesus

☐ I stop feeling pressured to prove myself good enough to escape God's judgment, and instead I take shelter only in Jesus. *His* righteousness protects me. "But now the righteousness of God has been manifested apart from the law, although the Law and the Prophets bear witness to it—the righteousness of God through faith in Jesus Christ for all who believe" (Romans 3:21–22).

❏ I hide behind the blood of Jesus, freed from nagging guilt, sure that every sin I've ever committed is fully covered by his infinitely valuable sacrifice. "By a single offering he has perfected for all time those who are being sanctified" (Hebrews 10:14).

❏ I lose the fear that God's fury is directed at me, and I believe that by faith in Jesus I now have a loving Father instead. "It is not the will of my Father who is in heaven that one of these little ones should perish" (Matthew 18:14).

Now share some of your choices with the group, and tell why those items are meaningful to you.

How might these habits make your wait for Jesus an *active* waiting, one where you are eager to join or support his mission to the world?

WRAP-UP AND PRAYER *10 MINUTES*

Pray for items from the exercise that you want to become true of you. Also pray about any personal frustrations or despair that your group has mentioned during this lesson. Pray that your waiting would be mercifully short, and also that you would learn to long for Jesus and to hope and hide in him.

MORE READING: If you are reading through all of Isaiah, read chapters 27 through 33 before the next lesson, which will be on chapters 34 and 35.

Lesson

5

THE WAY OF HOLINESS

BIG IDEA

We can take heart because God's everlasting judgment is coming upon our enemies and his everlasting salvation is coming to us.

BIBLE CONVERSATION *20 MINUTES*

In the chapters leading up to Isaiah 34 and 35, Isaiah urges the people of Jerusalem to trust God who will save them through judgment. So far, we've focused on how a form of judgment comes upon God's people. We've noted how the residents of Jerusalem will eventually go into exile in Babylon before being brought out on a joyful road trip home—which we'll see allusions to at the end of this lesson's passage. But the enemies God uses to chastise his people also deserve judgment. And in this passage, the focus is on how God's people are saved through their enemies' destruction.

The enemy mentioned by name is Edom, the descendants of Esau, who was the God-rejecting counterpart to his brother Jacob who fathered the Israelite people. Edom was the oldest and most consistently bitter enemy of God's people. Edom would even ally with Babylon in the slaughter and destruction at Jerusalem, and gloat

51

about it, so Isaiah singles out Edom as an example of what God will do to all enemies of his people. Edom is contrasted with Zion, another name for Mount Jerusalem, where God's people worship.

Have several readers take turns reading all of **Isaiah 34 and 35** aloud. Then discuss the questions below:

What words might describe the kind of judgment God's enemies receive in chapter 34, and how might this kind of judgment encourage God's people?

What words best describe the future God's people have in chapter 35, and how is this encouraging?

****

Continue by reading this lesson's article aloud, taking turns by paragraph. When you finish, discuss the questions that follow.

5

ARTICLE

JOY COMES IN THE MORNING

5 MINUTES

When I preached from this passage in Isaiah a few years ago, 276 schoolgirls had recently been kidnapped by anti-Christian terrorists in the town of Chibok, Nigeria. Meanwhile, in parts of the Middle East, Christians were facing a wave of genocide from militant factions, with families fleeing their homes to hide in the hills. Today, as I write this, many of the Chibok schoolgirls are still missing, and Christians in other parts of the world continue to face persecution for their faith—beaten, imprisoned, exiled, killed. And by the time you read this, new violence against believers surely will have broken out somewhere, maybe even where you live.

In many ways, this should not surprise us. Since the first sin in Eden, God's people have always been a persecuted people. God told the serpent, "I will put enmity between you and the woman, and between your offspring and her offspring" (Genesis 3:15). This stands as a towering text that casts a shadow over the rest of the Bible's storyline. On page after page, we read of violence and harassment and the killing of God's people by the devil's people—and life is no different today.

In the midst of such enmity, what do Christians long for? We look for a day of *reckoning* when wrongs will be *righted*. But more than that, we ache for freedom and a return home. We yearn for a day of *shalom*, when our world will be restored. Isn't that what the Chibok girls long for? They long for peace to replace persecution. And that's what Isaiah 34 and 35 give us.

In chapter 34, we have God's judgment on those involved in taking his people into exile. And then in chapter 35, we have God's salvation of his people as they return to the land. The two chapters must be read side by side, because for God's people to experience true and complete salvation, their enemy must experience complete destruction. If the Chibok schoolgirls escape from their captors, they wouldn't necessarily find true peace—because the men could return. Only if the evil men are destroyed can they enjoy real rest.

This is why "the LORD has a day of vengeance, a year of recompence for the cause of Zion. And the streams of Edom shall be turned into pitch, and her soil into sulfur" (34:8–9). We tend to recoil at this kind of talk. Aren't Christians meant to turn the other cheek? Aren't we meant to love our enemies? Well, yes, on a personal level. We are never to seek personal vengeance. But this is not because vengeance is wrong, but because it is not ours to seek—it is God's.

That's how these chapters about judgment-salvation serve a pastoral purpose. Do you see what is at the heart of God's vengeance? He acts "for the cause of Zion," the mountain where his people worship, which stood in part for the whole nation of Israel. This is not judgment for judgment's sake, but for God's people's sake. God will justly repay every person who has done his people wrong. And so, he will comfort his exiled and persecuted people who are living in a hostile world, that they may worship him in peace.

The imagery in chapter 34:5–6 is of a swordfight, meaning that God engages in person-to-person combat. This is God's *personal* vengeance, exacting individual punishment. He loves his people. He wants to preserve and save his people. He wants his people to prosper under his rule in a new Zion, and so his unclouded justice will avenge all true wrongs against them. All his bitterest enemies, who oppress his people, will become like a bloody desert. Those enemies may seem to be ruling at the moment, but our God will come personally to deal with them. That's the first word of comfort for exiled and persecuted Christians.*

The second word of comfort comes in chapter 35, where instead of a bloody desert God's people receive a blossoming desert. And with the renewed world comes a renewed people. The blind and deaf and lame are healed. Just as the first sin ruined both God's garden and his people, Jesus restores both the world and his people when he comes to save. He makes the world into a garden and heals us, making us ready to live in that new world.

All of this is so that we might find happiness in God: "And the ransomed of the LORD shall return and come to Zion with singing" (35:10). Look how we get there, on a highway called the Way of Holiness. That's not just a sinless road, it's a safe road. Nothing will be there that can harm God's people. Their return will be certain because of who they are. They are "the ransomed of the LORD." Verse 9 calls them "the redeemed."

Some highways are toll roads—you only get to use them if you pay. This highway is like a toll road, but with a difference: you can only get on it if someone else pays for you. That's what it means to be ransomed. And *redeemed* means a next-of-kin voluntarily pays the price to buy you back into the family. These terms are a picture of Christ, our Redeemer, our next-of-kin, who became

---

* See 2 Thessalonians 1:5–9

one of us in order to make us his brothers and sisters, sons and daughters of God.

People think holiness is boring, but look where this highway leads. Those who walk the Way of Holiness will be crowned with *everlasting joy*. All the sorrow and sighing of their exiled and persecuted life will flee away. Holiness always leads to happiness.

Today, many of the Chibok girls still know only unbroken sadness and trauma. Persecuted believers around the world still feel heartache and distress. But one day soon, they will all come to the heavenly Mount Zion with *everlasting joy* on their heads. Can you hear them singing?

DISCUSSION *10 MINUTES*

The article gave several reasons why vengeance is good when it comes from God. Which reason do you appreciate, and why?

What features of life on the Way of Holiness appeal to you, and why?

Lesson

EXERCISE

5

THE PRESENT HELP OF FUTURE HOPE

20 MINUTES

Some people might think that reading Bible passages about God's judgment will make you a believer bent on revenge, but it ought to do the opposite. Jesus's vengeance is more complete than yours ever could be, and his anger is perfectly right-minded—not mixed with selfishness like yours, but driven by concern for his people. When you know that Jesus surely is coming to bring judgment, you can let go of your anger and let him handle revenge. This frees you to be patient and loving even toward your enemies, praying that God in his mercy might one day make them your friends. Likewise, when you know that Jesus is coming to give you a perfected kingdom of eternal joy, you can let go of your greedy desires for this world's brief fame and fortune. You are freed to live humbly and generously.

This too is why the path of Jesus's kingdom is called the Way of Holiness. The future hope you have in Jesus's return helps you live with godly kindness and obedience today. In this exercise, you'll begin by working on your own to look at the connection between Jesus's return and how you live today. Then you'll share with the group.

First, read about Jesus's return. On your own, carefully read the two Bible passages below that tell how Jesus is coming to bring both vengeance and restoration. Mark, underline, or otherwise note some phrases you find encouraging, or eye-opening.

VENGEANCE: 2 Thessalonians 1:5–10. "This is evidence of the righteous judgment of God, that you may be considered worthy of the kingdom of God, for which you are also suffering—since indeed God considers it just to repay with affliction those who afflict you, and to grant relief to you who are afflicted as well as to us, when the Lord Jesus is revealed from heaven with his mighty angels in flaming fire, inflicting vengeance on those who do not know God and on those who do not obey the gospel of our Lord Jesus. They will suffer the punishment of eternal destruction, away from the presence of the Lord and from the glory of his might, when he comes on that day to be glorified in his saints, and to be marveled at among all who have believed."

RESTORATION: Revelation 21:3–5. "I heard a loud voice from the throne saying, 'Behold, the dwelling place of God is with man. He will dwell with them, and they will be his people, and God himself will be with them as their God. He will wipe away every tear from their eyes, and death shall be no more, neither shall there be mourning, nor crying, nor pain anymore, for the former things have passed away.' And he who was seated on the throne said, 'Behold, I am making all things new.'"

Second, think about the present help of your future hope. That is, consider how you are encouraged to live today because of what Jesus will do one day. Select at least one item below that you want to become true of you, or one you are thankful God is working in you:

❑ **Love.** I put aside hatred because I let Jesus be in charge of vengeance. I sacrifice my own comforts and preferences in this life because my reward is coming in the next life.

❑ **Generosity.** Unfair treatment doesn't make me bitter because I know Jesus will make the guilty pay. I spend my life giving, letting others go first, and praising others rather than myself—because my turn for glory will come.

❑ **Contentment.** I am patient and have an inner calm even when evil seems to win, since I know Jesus will destroy it one day. I am not jealous of the success, riches, or acclaim of others, because I live for greater pleasures.

❑ **Godliness.** Jesus's slaughter of evildoers and his tenderness toward the redeemed show me the stark contrast between wrong and right, between sin and godliness. I learn to hate sin and run from it, and to see the beauty of a holy life that stays near to Jesus.

❑ **Joy.** Even in a world of deep sorrows, I have an inner delight in Jesus—the destroyer of all makers of misery, and the restorer of all gladness. I am certain that when he comes, "sorrow and sighing shall flee away" (35:10).

❑ **Other:** _____.

When the group is ready, share some of your responses to both sections of the exercise, and explain why you chose them.

WRAP-UP AND PRAYER *10 MINUTES*

Pray for God to work holiness in you in particular areas of your life. If your group knows a prayerful song, you might consider singing it together in anticipation of the day when you will join all God's people coming into his city with joyful singing.

MORE READING: If you are reading through all of Isaiah, read chapters 36 through 39 before the next lesson, which will be on chapter 40.

6

COMFORT, COMFORT MY PEOPLE

BIG IDEA

We have comfort upon comfort because we have a forgiving, enduring, and incomparable God.

BIBLE CONVERSATION *20 MINUTES*

Starting with chapter 40, the audience Isaiah directly addresses skips forward about two centuries. The first half of the book spoke to the people of Jerusalem during the Assyrian threat, as judgment was looming but was delayed when God spared the city. Isaiah repeatedly confronted those people about their sin and told them of the judgment to come. The second half addresses later generations who are in exile in Babylon, living under that judgment, but who are about to return home or have recently arrived. Isaiah encourages them with the news of their salvation. In this way, the two halves of Isaiah are a big-picture version of the book's judgment-salvation rhythm.

Some have speculated that the second half of Isaiah was written by a later prophet to speak to the later generation, since how could Isaiah have known things two centuries ahead of his time, even naming Cyrus, king of Persia. However, the book never mentions a second prophet. And it is not a problem for God to know the future, since he declares "the end from the beginning and from ancient times the things not yet done" (46:10). The predictive elements in the second half of Isaiah's prophecy (mainly chapters 40–66) reflect not only the supernatural aspect of Isaiah's ministry but also its pastoral importance. What a great assurance to the people living in Isaiah's turbulent times to hear that God had so fully planned his coming judgment and salvation that he was already providing comfort to their descendants who would be in exile! And surely it was an equal comfort to the later exiles, as Jerusalem lay in rubble, to hear that God had foreknown their plight, pre-prepared their restoration, and informed them about it centuries in advance. Aren't we encouraged in the same way when we read how God planned our salvation in Jesus long before it happened and how he has told us already about the glory yet to come?

Have a volunteer read **Isaiah 40** aloud, or have several readers take turns. Then discuss the questions below:

The passage begins with a double decree of comfort. What do you find especially comforting in the words of this Isaiah 40?

Verse 9 tells of a herald announcing, "Behold your God!" Which of the pictures of God that follow do people especially need to see today, and why?

Look at the people's complaint in verse 27. What do you find helpful about the answer given in the rest of the chapter, and why?

* * * *

Next, take turns reading the article aloud, switching readers at each paragraph break. When you finish, answer the discussion questions.

Lesson

ARTICLE

DEEP COMFORT

5 MINUTES

When I was about five, my family and I were traveling through the Frankfurt airport in Germany. As we went through security, I took my eyes off my parents while everyone reclaimed their bags. Once people started to move again, I reached for the hand of the man beside me thinking it was my dad's. When I looked up and saw a strange man looking back at me, I started to cry. I searched for my dad but I couldn't see him, and for a very brief moment I felt *forgotten* and *forsaken*.

I was alone in a foreign country, listening to foreign voices, standing beside a man I didn't know. My dad quickly heard my cry and came and rescued me, but it was still a horrible experience at the time. Feeling forgotten and forsaken always is. And that's how God's people felt during their time in exile: "My way is hidden from the Lord, and my right is disregarded by my God" (v. 27).

And so, God's first words to his people who are about to come out of exile are, "Comfort, comfort my people." The double use of *comfort* conveys emotional intensity. But the words also are moving because the very God who brought the people under judgment for sin didn't break his personal bond with them. They are still *his* people. This is the good news of comfort: God does not forsake us even when we sin.

Of course, God does punish sin. That's why the people went into exile. It's why Jesus went to the cross. But once there is a payment for sin, God forgives. God comforts. The word *double*, where God says that Jerusalem has received "double for all her sins" (v. 2), is related to the word for folding something to produce two exact halves. It's like a paper folded so that one part perfectly covers the other. In other words, the punishment is full. It completely and exactly covers all our sin.

The people in exile were a picture of Christ on the cross. In Jesus, we see God's justice to completely and exactly punish every sin, and we see his mercy to forgive us by taking that punishment in our place. That's the deep comfort God offers sinners, available to anyone who wants it—justice and mercy, comfort upon comfort. I don't know what kind of day or week you've had sin-wise. But if your faith is in Jesus, hear God's word to you right now, spoken in light of the cross: "Comfort, comfort, my child. I speak tenderly to you that your iniquity is pardoned. Because your sin has been paid for completely and exactly."

Forgiveness is our first and great comfort, but there is more. There's also the comfort of God's enduring word, which is lasting and trustworthy even though we are fragile and fading like grass (v. 8). And there's the comfort of the Warrior-Shepherd, who comes with one arm raised to fight for us (v. 10) and the other arm tenderly caring for his little lambs (v. 11). That is how Jesus came, battling the world and sin and the devil while gathering and carrying his people, even taking babies in his arms.

But it's one thing to say all this about God and another for him actually to be able to do it. So Isaiah gives us yet another comfort: the comfort of a God who is beyond all comparison. The second half of Isaiah 40 contains some of the most breathtaking words about God in the whole book, if not the whole Bible. If you're ever feeling forgotten or forsaken, open up to this passage and read about your incomparable God.

God is beyond all measure. Isaiah pictures him using small-scale measuring tools—his hand, a basket, scales—to measure the world's extremes: oceans, mountains, coastlands, forests. God is also beyond all rivals. The idols of Babylon? They are deaf and mute and blind. The rulers of Babylon? God just "blows on them, and they wither" (v. 24). The stars seen in Babylon, where astrology was invented and where the stars were worshiped as an army of heavenly gods? God their Creator calls them out every night, each of them numbered and named. They march out to his orders and he switches them on.

Babylon's idols, Babylon's princes, Babylon's stars—none compare with God. They are grains of dust. And it's the same with our sins, our troubles, our oppressors. Can God redeem us and forgive us? Of course, he can; he's beyond all comparison. And here's the wonder: This God who holds the oceans in his hand came to us as a baby, held in the hand of a virgin girl. This God before whom the nations are a drop in a bucket allowed himself to be crucified by some Roman soldiers. This God beyond comparison took the form of a servant in order to save us.

Well, despite all this assurance of who God is, his people still don't feel comforted at the end of Isaiah 40. But notice how gently and personally he deals with them, using their name and his. "Why do you say, O Jacob, and speak, O Israel, 'My way is hidden from the LORD'?" (v. 27).

When your sin gets the better of you, or when life's troubles overwhelm you—when you feel forgotten and forsaken—remember that God knows your name and he calls you by name! He has named billions upon billions of stars, but he has also called *you* by name. That's what brought comfort to me that day in the airport. My dad came to me *calling my name*, and then he picked me up in his arms and carried me.

God's message to us is this: "I haven't forgotten you. I haven't forsaken you. I know your name. Look at the cross. I abandoned my own incarnate Son in the darkness so that you would never be forgotten or forsaken. Comfort, comfort my people."

DISCUSSION *10 MINUTES*

When in your life have you felt forgotten or forsaken by God?

How might your thinking about God need to grow, so that in your daily life you realize more of his greatness?

Lesson

EXERCISE

GOD'S MANY COMFORTS

20 MINUTES

Isaiah 40 describes God and his comforts so beautifully that it is worth reading repeatedly, slowly and carefully. You'll do that now with selected verses. On your own, begin this exercise by reading again what Isaiah says about some of the many comforts God gives. Read deliberately, noticing key words and phrases. Also think about situations in your life that call for God's comfort, and look for words and phrases that speak to you. Note those parts of the text, or underline them.

The comfort of FORGIVENESS

> Speak tenderly to Jerusalem,
>   and cry to her
> that her warfare is ended,
>   that her iniquity is pardoned,
> that she has received from the LORD's hand
>   double for all her sins. (v. 2)

The comfort of GOD'S ENDURING WORD

All flesh is grass,
>and all its beauty is like the flower of the field.
The grass withers, the flower fades
>when the breath of the Lord blows on it;
>surely the people are grass.
The grass withers, the flower fades,
>but the word of our God will stand forever. (vv. 6–8)

The comfort of GOD'S RULING ARM

Behold, the Lord God comes with might,
>and his arm rules for him;
behold, his reward is with him,
>and his recompense before him. (v. 10)

The comfort of the SHEPHERD

He will tend his flock like a shepherd;
>he will gather the lambs in his arms;
he will carry them in his bosom,
>and gently lead those that are with young. (v. 11)

The comfort of GOD'S WISDOM

Who has measured the Spirit of the Lord,
>or what man shows him his counsel?
Whom did he consult,
>and who made him understand?
Who taught him the path of justice,
>and taught him knowledge,
>and showed him the way of understanding? (vv. 13–14)

The comfort of an INCOMPARABLE GOD

> It is he who sits above the circle of the earth,
>> and its inhabitants are like grasshoppers;
> who stretches out the heavens like a curtain,
>> and spreads them like a tent to dwell in;
> who brings princes to nothing,
>> and makes the rulers of the earth as emptiness. (vv. 22–23)

The comfort of GOD'S GIFTS

> He gives power to the faint,
>> and to him who has no might he increases strength.
> Even youths shall faint and be weary,
>> and young men shall fall exhausted;
> but they who wait for the LORD shall renew their strength;
>> they shall mount up with wings like eagles;
> they shall run and not be weary;
>> they shall walk and not faint. (vv. 29–31)

Now think again about those situations in your life that call for comfort. Pick a few of the sentences below and complete them with one of the comforts found in Isaiah 40.

The comfort of _____
encourages me in a challenge I have at home or with my family, or in a personal crisis I'm facing.

The comfort of _____
helps me in a situation I face at work or in my daily activities.

The comfort of _____
strengthens me in a situation I'm dealing with at church, or in ministry or Christian service.

The comfort of _____ reassures me as I see troubling events in the world or in my community.

The comfort of _____
encourages me in my personal life with God.

When the group is ready, share and explain some of your responses.

WRAP-UP AND PRAYER *10 MINUTES*

As part of your prayer time together, thank God for his many comforts. Ask God to help you bring those comforts to mind when you are struggling with something in your life.

MORE READING: If you are reading through all of Isaiah, read chapters 41 through 48 before the next lesson, which will be on chapter 49.

7

YET I WILL NOT FORGET YOU

BIG IDEA

The beyond-compare love of God, and the engraved-in-flesh commitment of Jesus at the cross, mean that we his people will never be forgotten.

BIBLE CONVERSATION *20 MINUTES*

Following chapter 40's majestic celebration of God's sovereignty, Isaiah introduces two world leaders whom God uses to save his people:

- The first is Cyrus, a Persian king predicted in chapters 44–46 who will issue the edict allowing God's people to return to Jerusalem from exile. Cyrus is a mere human ruler who does not know the true God, yet God controls his decisions. Isaiah assures the people that God directs history, and that those who make history serve his will.

- The other is a person Isaiah calls the Lord's servant, first mentioned in chapter 42. This servant is a messiah figure who will do more than just bring the people back to their land; he will bring them back *to God*. He will lovingly save them from sin and extend God's rule to the whole world. The New Testament quotes several of Isaiah's servant passages, declaring that Jesus is this servant Isaiah announced centuries beforehand.*

This brings us to chapter 49, which begins with the Lord's servant (Jesus) speaking about his mission from God. Have someone read **Isaiah 49** aloud, or have several readers take turns, and then discuss the questions below:

In the servant's speech and God's response in verses 1–12, what traits of Jesus do you see that you find most attractive?

In verses 13–18, what do you appreciate about how God answers his people's doubts about the servant?

In verses 19–26, what will the servant accomplish that might encourage a weary missionary (or you, when you get discouraged in the Lord's work)? Explain.

---

* For example, Matthew 12:18–21; John 12:37–38; Acts 8:32–35.

****

Now read the article aloud, taking turns by paragraph. Then discuss the questions that follow.

THE MOST OFFENSIVE VERSE IN THE BIBLE

5 MINUTES

Isaiah 49 is a mountain-peak passage. Once you've climbed it, you just have to pause at the top and take in the view. So I want us to look at the summit of this passage, verses 14–16, because it gives us the most wonderful assurance that nothing in life could ever make God forget us.

Of course, that's not how the exiles in Babylon feel. God has just spoken of his coming servant who will restore his people and, even more, be a light for the nations "that my salvation may reach to the end of the earth" (v. 6). It's such good news that all creation rejoices: "Sing for joy, O heavens, and exult, O earth" (v. 13). But the people are still in captivity, far from home. To them, the good news might as well have been no news. "But Zion said, 'The LORD has forsaken me; my Lord has forgotten me'" (v. 14).

Notice how they address God first by his covenant name, the LORD. Yet they accuse the God who swears by his covenant name of breaking his covenant. Then they address God by his title, the Lord, a reference to his sovereignty. Yet they accuse the God who rules over everything of having forgotten something—his people.

Despite this, God responds not with browbeating or more exile, but with love and promise and reassurance.

> "Can a woman forget her nursing child,
>> that she should have no compassion on the son of her
>> womb?
> Even these may forget,
>> yet I will not forget you." (v. 15)

At first, we think the answer to God's rhetorical question must be obvious. No mother could ever forget her nursing child. It's the most intimate human relationship on earth. I remember a conference where the speaker told how, ten years before, he and his wife had a daughter born to them with a serious birth defect. She lived about an hour and then died in their arms. I was sitting next to his wife as he told the story, and I still remember seeing tears run down her face as he talked about it. It was ten years later, but that mother cried for her little girl like it was yesterday.

The heart of every mother cries out, "I could *never* forget my child!" That's what makes verse 15 one of the most offensive verses in the whole Bible. The text says, "Even these may forget." It does not say *some* mothers (the few, really bad mothers) might forget their children. No, it shockingly points out the ever-so-slight possibility that *any* mother might do the unthinkable.

There are places in the Bible where God's love is likened to that of a mother.* But here, God goes further. The point is that God's love is *not* like human love, not even like a mother's love. With a mother's love, even though we know that the chances of her ever forgetting her child are very, very slight, yet there still is the unthinkable possibility—offensive even to consider—that the seemingly impossible might happen, that she just might forget the child of her womb. Why? Because a mother's love is an imperfect, human love.

---

* See, for example, Isaiah 66:13; Matthew 23:37.

But God's love is wholly different: "Yet I will not forget you." It is impossible for God to forget his children. God is beyond comparison, and this includes his love. It is of a different order; it is in a league of its own—it is perfect love. And perfect love casts out fear, which is why we don't need to fear. God's love is steadfast, firm, immovable, unchanging in the storms of life.

And then in the next verse, God explains why he will not forget his children: "Behold, I have engraved you on the palms of my hands." Palms are *visible* as you go about your daily life. If you ever want to remember something you can write it on your hand and before long you will see it. Palms are also *intimate*. God marks a part of himself with our names—not painted on, but engraved. This involves scars, self-inflicted wounds.

And scarred palms also mean *condescension*. In the ancient Near East, a servant would have his master's name written on his hands. But here, the master is the Mighty One, the Holy One of Israel, the Incomparable One. This Lord condescends to have the name of his people written on his hands!

The rest of Isaiah 49 celebrates how God, when he remembers his people, goes on to bring the nations into his church and to conquer our enemies. He reassures his people that nothing will stand in the way of their restoration: not ruined walls, not bereavement, not kings and queens, not oppressors. In the same way, today he assures us that "neither death nor life, nor angels nor rulers, nor things present nor things to come, nor powers, nor height nor depth, nor anything else in all creation, will be able to separate us from the love of God in Christ Jesus our Lord" (Romans 8:38–39).

And how can we be sure of this? Because the God who said he has engraved us on the palms of his hands *actually did it*—in the person of Jesus Christ, the eternal Son, who condescended to demonstrate his love for us in five bleeding scars. God cannot forget us because

Jesus constantly intercedes for us, and he does so with scars on his hands. When Jesus looks at his scars in heaven, he thinks of you. When he was on the cross receiving those scars, you were on his mind. As he sits on his throne, you are still on his mind.

Today he says to you, "Can a woman forget her nursing child and have no compassion? Yes, maybe. But I will not forget you! My compassion is beyond compare. It is inextinguishable and inerasable. Look, I have engraved you on the palms of my hands!"

DISCUSSION *10 MINUTES*

When you read verse 15, about women forgetting their children but God not forgetting you, what emotional impact does it have on you?

How might you live differently if you had more confidence that God's love for you is unchanging, not wavering based on your behavior?

7

EXERCISE

WORRY OR ASSURANCE

20 MINUTES

God's assurance that he could not possibly forget his people is for you, if you have come to him to be saved by Jesus Christ. Jesus's love for you did not end at the cross, but is ongoing and inerasable, even when you sin. In heaven, Jesus is constantly praying for you, and once you are in his prayers it is impossible that he will ever forget you or give you up to sin and death.[3] Romans 8:33–35 says, "Who shall bring any charge against God's elect? It is God who justifies. Who is to condemn? Christ Jesus is the one who died—more than that, who was raised—who is at the right hand of God, who indeed is interceding for us. Who shall separate us from the love of Christ?"

Even when you know God says this, it can be hard to live as if you deeply believe it. So, on your own, read the descriptions in the chart below. They show the difference between a life of worry that God might forget you and a life of knowing that God remembers you. Pick out a few sets that remind you of your life or are ways you hope to grow. Be ready to share and explain your responses.

When I worry God might forget me . . .	When I know God remembers me . . .
I trust myself. I feel I must constantly earn God's love and salvation through right living, Christian service, and/or religious sincerity.	**I trust Jesus alone.** I rest in God's cannot-forget-me love, because nothing else is constant enough and strong enough to save me.
Life is a performance. My whole approach to God is manipulative, thinking I must convince him I'm good enough for him or serious enough about him.	**Life is resting in Jesus's performance.** My own appeals are unconvincing, but Jesus's blood and scars are the perfect plea on my behalf.
Jesus and salvation feel distant. My old sins haunt me and my new sins accuse me; they feel ever near me.	**Jesus and salvation feel near and now.** God's love is as sure as the scars of the cross which cannot be undone, and as present as Jesus's prayers for me which are happening at this moment.
Obeying God feels impossible. I try, but I keep failing, and I have little hope of real progress.	**I feel empowered to obey.** This very day, Jesus has been praying for me by name that I would be further cured of my selfishness and unbelief.
My sin weighs me down. I see how willingly my heart has pursued sin, and I doubt I can be forgiven.	**Jesus lifts me up.** I see how willingly Jesus's heart took him to the cross for me, how devotedly he follows through to defend me today, and how eagerly my Father already delights to forgive me due to his love beyond compare.
I am complacent. I figure some act of devotion on my part has (hopefully) already saved me, and now I lack eagerness to have God work faith and holiness in me every day.	**I am eager for more holiness.** It grieves me to sin against the God who loves me so fully, and I am hungry to become more faithful and holy.
My love for others is fake. When I do godly-looking acts, I am really trying to convince others, God, or myself that I am someone to admire.	**My love for others becomes real.** The sureness of Jesus's love for me frees me to love others and serve the church without an agenda.

When I worry God might forget me . . .	When I know God remembers me . . .
I serve God in my own strength. Unsure of God's favor, or that he's really willing to help, my ministry and/or fight against sin is marked by self-sufficiency.	**I serve God in his strength.** I work alongside God's Spirit, so I am regularly prayerful, teachable, and unafraid.
I act like an orphan. I am unsure I am loved, so I need to look out for myself.	**I act like a child of God.** I am sure of God's love and provision, so I am freed to care for others.
I feel Jesus is annoyed with me. I sin so often; it must exasperate him.	**I know Jesus is compassionate toward me.** Even my sins make him sympathize with my weaknesses and move him to help me (Hebrews 4:15).
My motivation to resist sin is weak. Deep down, it is based on little more than self-interest.	**My motivation to resist sin is strong.** It is based on love, gratitude, confidence that God is not fickle, and the joy of being like and being with my Savior.
I don't like telling about Jesus. Sharing my faith feels like a pressure-filled chore, and it quickly becomes drudgery.	**I'm eager to tell about Jesus.** I really am happy about him, and it gives me joy to tell others what God has done for me.

When the group is ready, share and explain some items that are meaningful to you. How has God been working in you? How would you like to grow?

WRAP-UP AND PRAYER *10 MINUTES*

Faith to believe what it true about Jesus is an ongoing challenge in the Christian life. Faith is a gift of God (Ephesians 2:8), so it's good to pray for it. Ask your loving Father to help you believe the good news about Jesus you've heard in this lesson.

MORE READING: If you are reading through all of Isaiah, read Isaiah 50:1–52:12 before the next lesson, which will start with Isaiah 52:13.

Lesson

8

MAN OF SORROWS

BIG IDEA

As believers in Jesus, our testimony is that we despised him but he loved us, we overlooked him but he carried our sorrows, and we were guilty but he bore our sin.

BIBLE CONVERSATION *20 MINUTES*

The climax of Isaiah's message about the Lord's coming servant occurs in chapter 53, which begins with a reference to "the arm of the LORD." That phrase ought to make us think of God's power to save his people during the original exodus, when he rescued them from Egypt "by trials, by signs, by wonders, and by war, by a mighty hand and an outstretched arm, and by great deeds of terror" (Deuteronomy 4:34). God flexed his biceps, so to speak, and the world shuddered.

But the bigger exodus, in which the servant (Jesus) saves the nations, will involve a very different-looking strength. Isaiah tells about it in an overview at the end of chapter 52 and then in four segments in chapter 53 that read like a testimony from witnesses who have come to believe in the servant. Have someone read **Isaiah 52:13–53:12** aloud, or have several readers take turns. Then discuss the questions below, one for each segment of the believers' testimony.

At first, the servant was despised by us (53:1–3). How do these verses fit your life before you became a believer in Jesus, or the attitude of others you've known?

The servant was punished because of us (53:4–6). Which parts of the believers' testimony about Jesus in these verses are most moving to you, and why?

The servant was innocent, unlike us (53:7–9). What might the fact that the servant is innocent yet remains silent reveal about his intentions and his moral character?

The servant did this to justify us (53:10–12). How are God, his people, and the servant all pleased with the outcome described in these verses?

* * * *

Now take turns reading the article aloud, switching readers with each paragraph. Then answer the discussion questions at the end of the article.

Lesson

ARTICLE

THE WEAK THINGS OF THIS WORLD

5 MINUTES

One of the earliest surviving pictorial representations of Jesus is a piece of graffiti from the third century.[4] The graffiti depicts a young man worshiping a donkey-headed figure on a cross. The inscription under the picture reads, "Alexamenos worships his God."[5] The graffiti seems to mock a Christian named Alexamenos for his faith in the crucified Christ.

It's how the world often thinks of the Christian faith—as a joke. Worshiping a man on a cross? What a laugh! In the Roman world, the cross spoke of guilt and shame and defeat—hardly things reasonable people would boast about! And yet, Christians do just that. We boast in the apparent foolishness of the crucified Christ. What looks preposterous to the world is wondrous to the believer.

That was the lesson God's people needed to learn in exile. The way God was going to rescue them was not how they would have imagined it. Already in Isaiah, God's announcement about Cyrus, the Persian king who would allow the people to return home, refers to him as "my shepherd" and "anointed one."* Those are titles reserved for King David and his royal line, not pagan

---

* Isaiah 44:28; 45:1.

84

Persians. And yet, God says this will be his saving way for Israel—an unexpected way that's not their way.

And so, for the Lord's servant who will bring the greater salvation, restoring his people to God by the Lord's mighty arm, what are they expecting? Will he be a triumphant figure who saves his people with public displays of power from on high? No, when the servant appears in Isaiah's prophecy, he is more puzzling than impressive.

- In chapter 42, the servant will bring justice to the nations but will do so in a way that's humble and quiet: "He will not cry aloud or lift up his voice, or make it heard in the street" (v. 2).

- In chapter 49, the servant is a light for the nations but also "deeply despised, abhorred by the nation, the servant of rulers" (v. 7).

- In chapter 50, the servant tells how he sustains the weary with his words but also lets himself be mistreated: "I hid not my face from disgrace and spitting" (v. 6).

And so the puzzle grows. By the end of chapter 52, the servant is high and exalted like a king one moment, but the next moment he's a marred man because of violence done against him. Yet this marred man will sprinkle the nations like a priest sprinkling blood on an altar to atone for people's sins; he will also stun kings into silence. The one mangled will be the one magnified. The one humbled will be the one exalted. And his exaltation will not come *in spite* of his suffering, but *because* of his suffering. He will succeed *through suffering*. His suffering is the arm of the Lord come to save his people!

Indeed, the testimony of the witnesses shows that a profound and powerful change has occurred in them. At first, they despised the servant. Even while he suffered for them, they considered him "smitten by God, and afflicted," as if he must have done *something* to deserve it. But then, with the eye of faith and the perspective of time, they—and we—see things differently: "But he was wounded for our transgressions; he was crushed for our iniquities" (53:5).

The language speaks of much more than just a violent death that might draw out sympathetic commitment from his followers. This servant's death was a punishment: he died to pay the penalty for the sins of his followers. It was also a substitution: "The LORD has laid on him the iniquity of us all" (v. 6). God was like a high priest, entering the fray and placing his hands on his servant's head, transferring all our sin to him.[6]

This makes the servant's death also an atonement, and it creates some irony. Now we realize the servant actually *was* smitten and afflicted by God—but not for his own sin. It was for our sin. To the outward eye, he was simply a man despised by us. But to the inward eye of faith, he was a man punished because of us, even though, unlike us, he was innocent.

These puzzling truths about the servant build on each other, culminating in *the* question about how our good God deals with evil: How could a God of justice enact punishment upon an innocent man in place of those who are guilty, and why would he do it? The answer is that he did it to justify us, to declare us no longer guilty of sin and to "make many to be accounted righteous" (v. 11).

Remember that the servant voluntarily, silently submitted himself to the crushing, and so removes any problem of injustice. The will of the Lord to crush his innocent servant was in fact the servant's own will to be crushed for the sins of his people. The servant willed what God willed. He loved those God loved. There is no tension here between a punishing God and a suffering servant—only harmony and mystery.

And, joy too. The servant's death would not be in vain: "Out of the anguish of his soul he shall see and be satisfied" (v. 11). In the end, the servant is portrayed as a living, victorious warrior dividing up the spoils of his bounty. And so, Isaiah's song about the servant ends where it began, with exultation—but only after suffering.

This is what distinguishes Jesus from other savior figures like Cyrus, the Persian king. Cyrus brought Israel back to the land at no personal cost to himself, but Jesus brings the nations back to God at great personal cost to himself. So hear the Father say to us, "Behold, my servant Jesus! The arm of the Lord veiled in weakness; the wisdom of God hidden in things despised." He may look foolish to the world, but we who are being saved are like Alexamenos. We bow and worship our God—crucified.

DISCUSSION *10 MINUTES*

How has salvation from sin through the cross of Jesus sometimes felt puzzling, troubling, or foolish to you?

How has your appreciation of Jesus's journey to the cross deepened your worship of him?

Lesson

EXERCISE

A TESTIMONY ABOUT JESUS

20 MINUTES

The four segments of Isaiah 53 make an excellent template for any believer's testimony. Whether it's to share with others or for personal reflection, it's good to think through what you confess to be true about yourself and about Jesus.

Begin by working on your own. For each item below, write a brief sentence to summarize a truth about yourself or Jesus that you might tell to others or ponder personally. Make your sentence something specific to you if you can, but it's also okay to write something general or to borrow a phrase from Isaiah 53 if you prefer that to writing your own. (If you aren't yet a believer, or aren't sure, there are probably still parts of Isaiah 53 you can appreciate, so complete as much of the exercise as you can.) When everyone is ready, you'll have a chance to share and explain some of your sentences.

At times, I have despised Jesus. For this item, you might:

- Tell how you used to live before you believed in Jesus.

- Tell something about Jesus that you still struggle with or are trying to understand.

- Share how, even though you now love Jesus, you still sometimes behave in ways that essentially reject or despise him.

- Write a personal sentence based on a line from verses 1–3, or copy a meaningful line from those verses.

_____

_____

_____.

Jesus was punished because of me. For this item, you might:

- Tell how it feels to have your sin forgiven.

- Tell what it's like to be loved so fully—all the way to the cross.

- Explain what you see in Jesus on the cross that you find worthy of worship.

- Write a personal sentence based on a line from verses 4–6, or copy a meaningful line from those verses.

_____

_____

_____.

Jesus was innocent, unlike me. For this item, you might:

- Tell something amazing about Jesus's life and character, or his treatment of you, that makes him beyond compare.

- Mention an area of life where you are encouraged to know that you get credit for Jesus's righteous record, not your own record.

- Write a personal sentence based on a line from verses 7–9, or copy a meaningful line from those verses.

_____
_____
_____.

Jesus has justified me. For this item, you might:

- Tell how it feels to be counted righteous in Jesus.
- Explain about one of the many "portions" or "spoils" Jesus has shared with you—some gift that's yours from him.
- Tell how Jesus makes your future bright.
- Write a personal sentence based on a line from verses 10–12, or copy a meaningful line from those verses.

_____
_____
_____.

When the group is ready, share some of your sentences. Explain why you think telling these things to others, or to yourself, might be helpful.

WRAP-UP AND PRAYER _10 MINUTES_

Follow up on the exercise by praying, both as a group now and on your own for the next week or two. Pray that God will bring someone along who needs to hear more about Jesus. If that person is open, share some part of your testimony with them. Make your goal not to push them for a decision or to get them to believe, but to love someone who does not yet know Jesus by telling them what he has done for you.

MORE READING: If you are reading through all of Isaiah, read chapter 54 before the next lesson, which will be on chapter 55.

9

COME TO THE WATERS

BIG IDEA

This world cannot satisfy any of our deepest longings, but God invites us to come to him and have them all filled in Jesus.

BIBLE CONVERSATION *20 MINUTES*

Having told about the Lord's Suffering Servant who will take the punishment for his people's sin, Isaiah celebrates the grace those people enjoy: God's compassion, his peace, and his unshakable covenant with them in which he is their loving God. Have someone read **Isaiah 55** aloud, or let a few readers take turns. Then discuss the questions below:

How have you labored "for that which does not satisfy" (v. 2), or how can you relate to the need to be more deeply satisfied?

In verses 3–7, how does God satisfy? Why might these things be deeply satisfying to you?

In verses 8–13, what assurances do you find that you really ought to come to God and will be satisfied?

****

Next, take turns reading the article aloud, switching readers at each paragraph break. Then discuss the questions that follow.

Lesson

ARTICLE

GOD WHO SATISFIES

5 MINUTES

Do you feel the urgency of Isaiah 55's invitation? Thirteen times God calls on us to do something: Come. Come. Come. Come. Listen. Delight. Incline your ear. Come. Hear. Seek. Call. Forsake. Return. The invitation is urgent, but at the same time it is joyful. The opening picture is of a banquet with wine and milk. God gets our taste buds flowing. He wants us to have our desires met. This is who he is—the God who satisfies our longings.

Of course, God does this with good things like food and wine and clothes and fun and games and exercise and sleep. But if we detach these gifts from the Giver, then our deepest longings will never be met. God himself is the only one who can fully satisfy us, and he gives us infinite love through his chosen king: "I will make with you an everlasting covenant, my steadfast, sure love for David" (v. 3).

King David was only ever a shadow of another, later king—the Suffering Servant-King, Jesus. If we want to be truly satisfied, we need to come to King Jesus and enter the everlasting covenant with him. When Isaiah probes behind our dissatisfaction, he finds our root problem—sin. But Jesus offers us forgiveness for it. This is why the joyful invitation includes the two-sided call to repent: to forsake our own ways, and "return to the LORD." When we do, "he will abundantly pardon." When we repent, God meets us not with a frown but with a smile.

The American preacher Arnold Prater tells the story of an old, profane barber who enjoyed being especially vulgar whenever the preacher came into his shop. During a brush with death, the barber turned in desperation to God and sensed God answering. Afterward he told Prater, "Oh preacher, I've kicked him in the face every day of my life for sixty years and for the first time in my life I called his name and he came."[7] That's what Isaiah is saying. Come, seek the Lord. Whatever you've done with your life, you'll find him full of forgiveness.

To encourage us to seek the Lord for full forgiveness, Isaiah gives us two reasons in two illustrations. The first is that God's ways and thoughts are higher than ours, "as the heavens are higher than the earth" (v. 9). There's a heaven-and-earth difference between God and us. And this isn't just a moral or intellectual difference. Isaiah connects it to the Lord's compassion and abundant forgiveness.

Isaiah wants us to see the way God deals with sinners is not like our way, and the way God thinks about sinners is not the way we think. The human way is finger-pointing, revenge, punishment, bitterness, and grudges. Our default position is condemnation. But God's default position is mercy and forgiveness. It's his lifestyle and mindset.

The second reason to seek the Lord for full forgiveness is because his word is not like our word. Isaiah's illustration here is rain and snow. When rain falls, it satisfies us with good things—seed to sow and bread to eat. Rain can't help but produce this intended purpose. It *always* causes things to grow.

It's the same with God's word. God says, "It shall not return to me empty, but it shall accomplish that which I purpose" (v. 11). The "word" here is the word of invitation to come to God for true satisfaction and full forgiveness. When God declares satisfaction and forgiveness, it never comes back to him empty. Our own promises are so often well-intended but just become hot air. God's word is never like that. In creation, God spoke and it was so. And in the gospel, God speaks and it is so, which means that if we repent, he *will* forgive us. His word is as good as the rain that waters the earth—it never returns empty.

That's because this word is about the living Word, the Servant-King who became flesh and dwelt among us. Jesus is God's last Word spoken to us, and that Word did not return to God empty-handed. Jesus accomplished all that God intended: complete forgiveness for sinners like you and me. God is true to his word and he is true to Jesus. He will forgive.

The chapter finishes with a picture of a new Eden. Along with the joy and peace Jesus gives us, there's a whole-world change. It's as if the physical creation is bursting at its seams to celebrate what occurs in our lives. Mountains sing, trees clap, and thorns give way to evergreen trees. And this combination—a new people, forgiven and satisfied, in a new creation—will make God famous: "It shall make a name for the LORD" (v. 13). He will be famous for his grace.

For all eternity, God will be seen to be the kind of God he is: a God who, after people punched him, and spat on him, and crucified him, said, "Forgive them, forgive them." He's the kind of God who, when you kick him in the face all your life and then call his name, comes to you and says, "I forgive you."

He is speaking to us, right now. "Seek me while I may be found. Buy wine and milk for free." Rich foods like fine wine and creamy milk are never actually free, but they can be free if someone else is paying. Your forgiveness cost Jesus his life. He's made the payment. Now he makes the invitation: Come. Seek. You *will find*. God wants to be found by you.

DISCUSSION *10 MINUTES*

What would it look like for you to answer God's invitation to come to him, either for the first time or as part of your ongoing life with him?

Forsaking your own ways and returning to God can feel hard, like you are losing your very self (the Bible calls it death to self). How has it also been joyful and satisfying to you?

Lesson

EXERCISE

FINDING SATISFACTION

20 MINUTES

In the Bible, one of the many faces of sin is dissatisfaction. Sin only ever dissatisfies. We can see this in every culture. People long to find satisfaction in fame, wealth, reputation, work, family, sex, or other desires. But even if we seem to get these things we still aren't satisfied, because we're looking in all the wrong places. Psalm 42:2 says, "My soul thirsts for God, for the living God," but our sinful tendency is to look for joy in everything and anything *but* God.

For you to find true joy in God, it helps to identify the false gods you tend to think can satisfy you. For each category, work on your own to pick from the list some false satisfiers that are especially tempting for you, or have been. Many of them might be good things—even gifts from God—but they become sinful replacements for God if you seek satisfaction in them rather than in the giver. Then consider how God's certain and dependable word to you can help you turn instead to him. Note or underline some phrases in each Bible passage that might encourage you. At the end of the exercise, you'll be able to share some of your responses with the group.

Approval and acclaim. I look for satisfaction in the recognition and respect I get from others.

❑ At work or in my career

❑ Within my family or marriage, or for having a good family

❑ In my ministry or church involvement

❑ In my social circles

❑ By reaching a level of fame, notoriety, or notice

❑ For my appearance, demeanor, or abilities

❑ Other: _____

God's word to you says that, united to Jesus by faith, you enjoy the approval and righteous reputation that really counts and really lasts—the approval of God: "The fear of man lays a snare, but whoever trusts in the LORD is safe. Many seek the face of a ruler, but it is from the LORD that a man gets justice" (Proverbs 29:25–26).

Impact and achievement. I look for satisfaction in being able to make a noticeable difference or leave a legacy.

❑ In the world and my community, or through important causes

❑ In the church and God's kingdom

❑ In my work or daily activities

❑ In my family or the lives of those I love

❑ Other: _____

God's word to you says all creation is eagerly waiting to see your better legacy, the one you enjoy as a person Jesus has ransomed:

"Worthy are you to take the scroll
and to open its seals,

for you were slain, and by your blood you ransomed
people for God
from every tribe and language and people and nation,

and you have made them a kingdom and priests to
our God,
and they shall reign on the earth." (Revelation 5:9–10)

Love and attention. I look for satisfaction in being appreciated and loved.

❏ Within my family, marriage, or other close relationship

❏ Within my social circles

❏ At work, in ministry, or in other activities of my life

❏ Other: _____

God's word to you says that, in Jesus, you have a love from God that is beyond compare, and your experience of it will only get better and richer: "God, being rich in mercy, because of the great love with which he loved us, even when we were dead in our trespasses, made us alive together with Christ—by grace you have been saved—and raised us up with him and seated us with him in the heavenly places in Christ Jesus, so that in the coming ages he might show the immeasurable riches of his grace in kindness toward us in Christ Jesus" (Ephesians 2:4–7).

Comforts and wealth. I look for satisfaction in things that offer security and prosperity.

❏ Money or financial stability

❐ Health or safety

❐ Comforts that come with where I live, the people I know, and the belongings I can acquire

❐ Some kind of prosperity or success for those I love

❐ Other: _____

God's word to you says none of these things of the world will last for long, but Jesus and the riches of heaven are forever: "Do not lay up for yourselves treasures on earth, where moth and rust destroy and where thieves break in and steal, but lay up for yourselves treasures in heaven, where neither moth nor rust destroys and where thieves do not break in and steal" (Matthew 6:19–20).

Redemption. I look for satisfaction in recovering a sense that I have made things right, fixed troubles, or atoned for hurts and failures.

❐ For hurts and wrongs I've done to others, that weigh on me

❐ For hurts and wrongs done to me, that have distressed or damaged me

❐ For persistent sadness, disappointment, anger, or regret in my life

❐ For ways I feel like a failure or have had my hopes dashed

❐ For ways I feel a need to prove myself

❐ Other: _____

God's word to you says that, because of Jesus and only in him, your hurts and sins and failures will indeed be irretrievably buried and forgotten forever: "He will again have compassion on us; he will tread our iniquities under foot. You will cast all our sins into the depths of the sea" (Micah 7:19).

Enjoyments and escapes. I look for satisfaction in things that entertain me or that offer pleasure or escape.

☐ Diversions and amusements

☐ The ability to relax, enjoy recreations, or keep up a favored lifestyle

☐ Sexual enjoyments

☐ Food and/or drink

☐ Social escapes and enjoyments

☐ Other: _____

God's word to you says the escape you need is a remade world where Jesus reigns—an enjoyment of life with him that begins now and will soon be perfected: "Delight yourself in the Lord, and he will give you the desires of your heart" (Psalm 37:4). "You have sorrow now, but I will see you again and your hearts will rejoice, and no one will take your joy from you" (John 16:22).

When the group is ready, share some of your responses. Where besides God do you tend to look for satisfaction? What assurances from God might help you turn to him?

Think about these particular lures in your life and consider again: What will it look like, in your life, for you to forsake your own ways and return to God?

WRAP-UP AND PRAYER *10 MINUTES*

As part of your prayer time together, ask your loving Father to give you a thirst for him, a repentant heart, and confidence in his word. As you ask, be aware that he loves to have you come to him and delights to give you all that is good.

MORE READING: If you are reading through all of Isaiah, read Isaiah 56:1–65:16 before the next lesson, which will start with Isaiah 65:17.

10

NEW HEAVENS AND NEW EARTH

BIG IDEA

In Christ, our coming life will feature shared joy with God and a reversal of the losses and distresses of this world.

BIBLE CONVERSATION *20 MINUTES*

As Isaiah nears the end of his book, chapter 65 features the Lord speaking to his people. He begins by recalling some of their old struggles and acknowledging their current struggle of living in the midst of unbelieving nations. But then God declares a new heavens and new earth in which these troubles will be reversed and forgotten. Although the Lord's servant who was prominent in earlier chapters is not mentioned directly, he is there in the background. Everything in this new creation is a result of his work. Have someone read **Isaiah 65:17–25** aloud. Then discuss the questions below:

In verses 17–19, what details about the joy that will mark the new heavens and new earth catch your attention, and why?

Of all the ways the new heavens and new earth will be different from our current world, which do you think you might appreciate most, and why?

What have you learned from your study of Isaiah, and how does this passage add to it?

* * * *

Now read the final article aloud, switching readers by paragraph. Then discuss the questions at the end of the article.

THE CURSE IN REVERSE

5 MINUTES

In C. S. Lewis's *The Lion, the Witch and the Wardrobe*, Aslan the Lion dies at the hands of the White Witch for treachery committed by the boy Edmund. But the next day, Aslan suddenly appears alive and well. He explains that the witch didn't know about the magic planned before time: that when a willing victim who had committed no wrong was killed in a traitor's stead, "Death itself would start working backward."[8]

That idea of death itself working backward captures what Isaiah 65 is all about. This passage is about the reverse of the curse God pronounced after the first sin in Eden. Death was a central part of that great curse, and all through this passage there are reminders of death. Isaiah mentions weeping, distress, an infant who lives but a few days, a man who doesn't survive into old age, and a wolf and lamb together. Don't wolves kill lambs?

And yet, the passage is not about death, but life. It's about the world to come, the new heavens and the new earth where there will be no more death. It's about how the curse, with death as its main symbol, is worked all the way back to life and family and fellowship and peace. "The former things shall not be remembered or come to mind" (v. 17).

God is going to create everything anew. It will be so new that all the old marks and stains and dents of sin, and its effects in this world, will be completely removed in the world to come. Death will not get a mention in the new creation. We will not spare it a thought, because gladness and joy will fill our minds and crowd out all the former things. God actually says, "I create Jerusalem to be a joy, and her people to be a gladness" (v. 18). Gladness and joy will become our identity, the very core of our nature.

But I find the next thing God says to be even lovelier: "I will rejoice in Jerusalem and be glad in my people." Understand that the Bible calls God the blessed God. He is already the happiest being in the universe, and he doesn't need anything or anyone else to make him happy. He is self-sufficient, not dependent on us for his happiness—if he were, he would not be God. And yet, here is the happy God finding happiness in us! Here is God's heart being made glad by his people.

It's an astonishing thought, reminding me of Zephaniah 3:17, where God says he will rejoice over us with gladness and exult over us with loud singing. Heaven is going to be amazing when we hear the multitude of saints singing, and when we hear angels singing. But imagine when we hear God sing! And what's he going to sing about? You and me. We will have put a new song in God's heart. In this life we can "grieve" God, but in the next life we will only "gladden" him.[9]

God's reason for rejoicing over us is that all weeping and cries of distress will be gone from us. God is going to eliminate the sin that causes our sorrows and sighing. He will rejoice in his people because the root of all their groans and cries will be eliminated forever. The rest of the passage describes what we're going to enjoy as God's renewed people in his new creation. It's what's going to make God rejoice over us with singing:

- We will enjoy long and certain life in which death cannot touch us because sin is no longer present.

- We will have secure and satisfying life in which our homes and livelihoods cannot be lost and our work is never futile or disappointing.

- We will find fulfillment in a family life in which sin and death cannot interrupt the blessing of God that flows through the generations of his people.

- We will enjoy perfect and immediate fellowship with God in which nothing can hinder our calling and his answering.

- We will live in total and permanent peace in which old hostilities cease.

The final hostile creature named in Isaiah 65 is the serpent: "Dust shall be the serpent's food" (v. 25). He is mentioned last because he is our first enemy, the original cause of all sin and death. This is a picture of the final destruction of the devil, promised by God immediately after that first sin.* What creature can survive by eating dust? This is the permanent removal of the devil's influence on the world. It is hostility worked backward into harmony. It is the rule of the serpent worked backward into the rule of God.

All this is possible because of the person who crushed the serpent, the Suffering Servant-Messiah, Jesus Christ. When Jesus died, the graves of some saints were opened and their bodies raised from the dead.** Right then, the curse began to rewind because Jesus had absorbed it in our place.

---

* See Genesis 3:14.
** See Matthew 27:52.

On the cross, Jesus was winning for us the new heavens and new earth by receiving all the sorrows of our sin-cursed earth. He undid death, but only by dying. He overcame futility, but only because he felt like he'd spent his strength in vain. He blessed his offspring (that is, his spiritual family) by winning life for us, but only because he was cut off. He restored our fellowship with God, but only because he called to God and God did not answer. He won for us permanent peace, but only by suffering the serpent's bite himself.

Where does the new creation and a renewed people begin? Where is it won? On a bloody cross, by the Suffering Servant who puts the curse into reverse. This is how God is turning our weeping into a glad song—our song and his.

DISCUSSION *10 MINUTES*

Why might it be helpful for you to be reminded that your joy and Jesus's joy are compatible and occur together?

When you realize that Jesus has already begun putting the curse into reverse, how might it encourage you to work for his kingdom or his mission to the world?

WHAT HAVE YOU LOST?

20 MINUTES

Life in the current world is so full of loss and suffering that you might have a hard time even imagining what the new creation will be like. One way to appreciate a passage like Isaiah 65 is to begin by thinking about the losses you've experienced in this life, or about things you worry you might lose.

On your own, read through the items below, which are drawn from our passage. They describe losses you may have experienced and how Jesus will reverse them in the new creation. Pick one that fits you, and get creative. Write a few sentences that describe your loss and the reversal Jesus is working. You might choose to write as if you were making a journal entry, or you might create a few lines of poetry, or some other form of writing. Or if you prefer, draw pictures to describe your loss and the reversal. When you're done, you'll have a chance to share your writing or your pictures.

> **LOSS: Death or the shortness of life.** You have experienced sadness and loss due to death, or you are troubled by the prospect of death.

REVERSAL: God declares that death will not exist in his world. He will swallow up death so that it completely loses any of its past, present, or future power over you, and he will wipe away every tear you have wept over it. "No more shall there be in it an infant who lives but a few days, or an old man who does not fill out his days" (v. 20).

LOSS: Destroyed or long-gone places, possessions, or cherished times. You are sad about a period of life you can't get back, dear people or possessions you can't recover, or a sense of home and belonging that's now missing from your life or soon will be.

REVERSAL: God promises an end to all insecurity and upheaval, and to the worry and grief you feel because of them. Everything good will last, and you will be satisfied. "They shall build houses and inhabit them; they shall plant vineyards and eat their fruit" (v. 21).

LOSS: Futility in work, ministry, or home life. You are discouraged over how your hard work has failed to produce the results you wanted, or you kick yourself over how your own sin and missteps have ruined things.

REVERSAL: God says you will enjoy your work and your relationships, and will find them fulfilling and fruitful. "They shall not build and another inhabit; they shall not plant and another eat; for like the days of a tree shall the days of my people be, and my chosen shall long enjoy the work of their hands" (v. 22).

LOSS: Wayward, embittered, or absent family members or friends. You grieve over hurts and regrets having to do with those closest to you, whom you love.

REVERSAL: God assures you of a world where those you love will also share in his covenant love—where grace will run in the family, and where sin and death cannot interrupt the blessing that flows through the generations. "They shall not labor in vain or bear children for calamity, for they shall be the offspring of the blessed of the LORD, and their descendants with them" (v. 23).

LOSS: A sense of distance from God. Your sin and frustrations, and the distractions of life, keep you from praying or remaining close to God, so that you rarely enjoy him or feel confident that he delights in you.

REVERSAL: God says your frustrations and interruptions will give way to unhindered, immediate, and joy-filled fellowship with him. Your days of avoiding God, or thinking time with him is boring, will be gone forever. Your heart and his will be in perfect sync. "Before they call I will answer; while they are yet speaking I will hear" (v. 24).

LOSS: Animosity and ongoing bad will. People have hurt you or you have hurt others, and there is irreparable hate or hostility because of it, and it weighs on your life—or you are simply tired of seeing and fighting evil in yourself and in the world.

REVERSAL: God declares an end to old hostilities where one of his creatures hurts another. You will enjoy total and permanent peace. "The wolf and the lamb shall graze together; the lion shall eat straw like the ox, and dust shall be the serpent's food. They shall not hurt or destroy in all my holy mountain" (v. 25).

Now be creative. Pick a meaningful item above and write or draw about it. (If you don't feel creative, that's okay. Just pick a few words or phrases from an item above and reflect on them, and be ready to share some of your thoughts.)

When the group is ready, share some of what you wrote or drew. What losses have you experienced, and how does God's promise of the new creation encourage you?

WRAP-UP AND PRAYER *10 MINUTES*

Before you end your time together, your group might discuss how you can continue to encourage each other with the message of Isaiah and how you can keep praying for each other.

MORE READING: If you are reading through all of Isaiah, finish by reading chapter 66 on your own.

MORE STUDY: If you wish to move forward from Isaiah by studying further the period of Israel's return from exile, one good resource would be the companion study in the series, *Ezra and Nehemiah: Restoring the Ruins* by Iain M. Duguid (Greensboro, NC: New Growth Press, 2022).

LEADER'S NOTES

These notes provide some thoughts and background information that relate to the study's discussion questions, especially the Bible conversation sections. The discussion leader should read these notes before the study begins. Sometimes, the leader may want to refer the group to a point found here.

However, it is important that you not treat these notes as a way to look up the "right answer." The most helpful and memorable answers usually will be those the group discovers on its own through reading and thinking about the Bible text. You will lose the value of taking time to look thoughtfully at the text if you are too quick to turn to these notes.

LESSON 1: REDEEMED BY JUSTICE

In Isaiah 1, God describes many sides to his people's sin. Outwardly, they are violent (v. 21), corrupt (v. 23), and uncaring about the needy (v. 23). They don't repent of this because inwardly they are rebellious (v. 2), hardhearted (vv. 5–6), and shameless (vv. 28–30). God is particularly displeased by their hypocrisy: they continue to go through the motions of worship even though they clearly do not love what God loves (vv. 11–17).

Your group might notice that, in verse 17, God brings up what we call *social justice*. In recent years, many Bible-believing Christians have not known what to do with social justice. We are nervous to talk about it and nervous to do it. We've seen good people and good churches veer off the road into the ditch of the "social gospel," where social agendas push aside the gospel of salvation in Christ, or where worldly definitions of justice overrule God's greater justice. Indeed, that is a ditch we must avoid at all costs.

But there is also a ditch on the other side of the road—the ditch of religiosity and hypocrisy. We should not religiously attend our worship services and weekly prayer meetings but then be socially unconcerned the rest of the time. James tells us that pure and undefiled religion is taking care of widows and orphans (James 1:27). The social justice commands in the Bible (and there are many of them) are grounded in God's redemptive acts of rescuing Israel from its own oppression and slavery, and in how God has rescued us from the oppression of sin. Concern for others who are oppressed and helpless is part of the fabric of life for God's people because at one time it was us who were needy, and God helped us. In this way, it is welded to the true gospel of Jesus.

However, social concern clearly cannot be the gospel itself, and "redeemed by justice" in verse 27 surely means something different than social action. Just look at the blessings that come to God's people: absolute forgiveness (v. 18), fatherly care and prosperity (v. 19), renewed hearts that repent and trust God (vv. 25–27), worldwide worship (2:2–3), and lasting peace (2:4). Only through the judgment suffered by Jesus do we get such a full salvation and such complete justice.

LESSON 2: HOLY, HOLY, HOLY

There is nothing small, or even remotely approachable, about God as Isaiah sees him. The vision already is a revelation of God accommodated to Isaiah's mind, since no one can see God in his bare essence and live (Exodus 33:20). But even in this accommodated form, God is so highly exalted and so spectacularly immense that Isaiah can only describe the fringe of what God is wearing—the train of his robe, which fills the temple so that Isaiah cannot think of coming near. Even with God hidden in smoke, the seraphim cannot so much as look at him. Their conduct underscores their creatureliness and his utter holiness as the only Creator God, glorious not only in his temple but in all the world. The Lord is no domestic deity, at home in heaven but largely absent elsewhere. No, all the world is full of his transcendent majesty and his moral purity.

Isaiah's response is a cry of *woe*—a word tied to the Bible's curses (for example, see 1 Samuel 4:7–8; Isaiah 3:9–11; Matthew 23:1–36). Isaiah sees that he is lost, a man of unclean lips. This is more than just being lost for words. Lips reveal hearts. The lostness Isaiah sees and feels comes from having his heart exposed by the majesty of God. This exposure of the heart is typically the first blessing of grace God gives to his people. Then, with their self-absorption undone, he deals with the sinful core they have come to see. Modern psychology and pop religion try to reintegrate a person without any reference to sin and guilt and God's curse, which is only a superficial fix. But Jesus fully addresses all the pain of sin and guilt, atoning for it on the cross, and then reintegrates the whole person in the service of God.

At first glance, Isaiah's mission might not sound enjoyable. He will be speaking words of judgment to people who will not listen. But those of us familiar with the Bible's whole story also realize that he will be speaking words about Jesus, the timeless King he saw on the throne in his vision (see John 12:41). In the end, through the Bible, many believers from every nation will hear Isaiah's words and take them to heart, and will join the thundering circle around their Lord's throne.

LESSON 3: A SHOOT FROM THE STUMP OF JESSE

Do not overlook the fact that the description of the coming king begins with the encouraging word that "the Spirit of the LORD shall rest upon him" (11:2). This is a biblical pattern in godly leaders who are true game changers. Samson needed the Spirit to rush upon him in order to show his strength (Judges 14:6), and Saul and David were anointed with the Spirit in order to perform their kingly office (1 Samuel 10:10; 16:13). So too, Jesus had the Spirit's anointing for his earthly ministry (Luke 3:22; 4:1, 14–19). This is the God-given source of all the character qualities Isaiah describes: the king's justice, moral rectitude, righteousness, faithfulness to God, and opposition to evil.

The coming world the king will bring in is too perfect to be our current world, and we may have trouble even imagining it. Power will no longer dominate weakness (the lamb invites the wolf for dinner). Danger will no longer threaten the young (a child leads them). Hostile natures will no longer even exist (the lion eats straw).[10] This passage's snake imagery brings to mind our greatest nemesis, the devil (see 2 Corinthians 11:3; Revelation 12:9). He too will no longer threaten or tempt us, which is a freedom unknown to us in this life.

The Bible treats the original exodus from Egypt as a preview of Jesus's saving work. Luke 9:31 uses *exodus* (translated "departure" in the ESV) to summarize Jesus's death and resurrection in Jerusalem (see also Matthew 2:13–15; 1 Corinthians 10:1–4; Hebrews 3:1–4:10). The first exodus rescued God's people from physical slavery; the greater exodus rescues us from spiritual slavery (Romans 6:6). The first exodus buried Pharaoh; the greater exodus crushes Satan (Romans 16:20). The first exodus made a highway out of Egypt for Israel; the greater exodus is worldwide— it brings believers out of every nation and into the kingdom of Christ (Mark 13:24–27; Colossians 1:13).

LESSON 4: THE DESIRE OF OUR SOUL

The city of God in Isaiah's song is secure, with strong walls and bulwarks. It is welcoming, with open gates. And it is peaceful, with its foundation an everlasting rock—God himself. The rock is an architectural point, something to build on. The picture shows how God is someone totally dependable to build our lives upon. Just as we feel safe inside a solidly built house, we can enjoy perfect peace trusting God. God's people in this song are marked by faith (26:2), mindfulness about God (v. 3), and a deep desire for God (v. 8). These are spiritual traits God honors.

In contrast, the lofty city of man is proud and in defiance against God. The wicked in this song don't learn from God's goodness to them (v. 10) nor see his work in the world (v. 11). And so, their future is to be laid low, with even the poor and needy trampling over them.

But from our vantage point in this fallen world, the unmeasurable difference between the end for God's people and the end for the wicked is not yet seen. Because the whole world is fallen, we all live in cities that are under God's curse and judgment for sin. For this reason, God's people are eager to heed his personal call to come inside and shut their doors until his fury has passed by (v. 20). The words *come* and *enter* recall God's words to Noah, whom he shut inside the ark (Genesis 7:1–16). And the picture of going indoors until God's anger has passed by recalls the Passover in Egypt (Exodus 12:7–13). Both were judgment events—and in both, God saved his people by sheltering them in the midst of the storm of his wrath. Today, he does the same for us, sheltering us from his coming day of wrath when we take shelter in Jesus.

LESSON 5: THE WAY OF HOLINESS

The fighting between the devil's people and God's people is a major theme in Scripture. We see it from the start in Cain's aggression against Abel (Genesis 4), and it continues all the way to the life of

Jesus. The Pharisees, the Romans, and King Herod (an Edomite) all persecute Jesus and eventually go after his followers. If your group asks, "Didn't Jacob and Esau make peace in Genesis?" point out that the peace did not last. Edom attacked Israel on its way into the promised land (Numbers 20:14–21), and the hostility continued afterwards. For background on the destruction God promised Edom because of its rub-it-in complicity with Babylon, see Psalm 137, Jeremiah 49:7–22, Ezekiel 25:12–14, and the book of Obadiah.

The judgment God enacts in chapter 34 is bloody and severe (v. 3). It is a personal act of God (vv. 5–6). In a sense, it is a sacrifice, with God claiming the devotion due him that was not freely given (vv. 6–7). It is a judgment that lasts forever (v. 10). And unlike the partial judgment God's people endure, this judgment on his enemies leaves those enemies with no hope or inheritance. Their land becomes the permanent home of wild animals (vv. 11–17).

But while God's enemies experience death and disintegration, his saved people experience life and rejuvenation. Chapter 35 personifies the desert as singing and rejoicing to the beat of salvation. The places named in verse 2 are known for their beauty, but the greater beauty will be the glory of the Lord. Jesus gave us a glimpse of this coming glory during his earthly ministry. The blind and deaf and lame whom he healed were a sign of his kingdom's arrival (see Luke 7:18–28), which he will complete when he returns. Isaiah pictures a fully rejuvenated future, both entirely holy and completely happy—two qualities always found together.

LESSON 6: COMFORT, COMFORT MY PEOPLE

Isaiah 40 begins with a picture of God coming to save his people, crossing valleys and leveling mountains to get to them. So, it should not surprise us that this passage gives us multiple previews of the God who came to us in Jesus—especially since the Gospels themselves quote verse 3 to announce his arrival (see Matthew 3:3; Mark 1:3; Luke 3:4; John 1:23). Your group might notice many ways this chapter not only reveals God's glory but points to Jesus who would reveal it in more fullness (John 1:14).

Here is the God who comes to comfort sinners; just think of the way Jesus ate with prostitutes and greedy tax collectors—not to endorse their lifestyle, but because he knew that their sin made them guilty and miserable and he wanted to offer them forgiveness (Matthew 9:10–13). Here is the God who comes with might; just think of the way Jesus caused demons to fall down before him (Luke 8:28). Here is the God who tends his flock like a shepherd; just think of the way Jesus saw the crowds and had compassion on them (Matthew 9:36). Here is the God who can measure the oceans and the heavens with his hand; just think of the way Jesus spoke to the wind and the waves and they became still (Mark 4:39). Here is the God who was so great the forests of Lebanon and all its animals could not make enough wood and meat for a sacrifice suitable for him; just think of the way Jesus came and made himself the perfect sacrifice that paid for our sin.

LESSON 7: YET I WILL NOT FORGET YOU

Isaiah 49 gives a picture of God's servant being called, from before he was born, to a unique and global mission. Much of what we see here we will also see in Jesus's life described in the Gospels and in his purpose explained in the rest of the New Testament: He is a servant faithful to his God-given mission to teach and rescue the people even when the people are less than cooperative and the mission involves suffering (vv. 2–4). He is reliant on God and honored by God (v. 5). He is for all people and nations (vv. 6–7). He is a gift to the people, representing them in their covenant with

God and earning an inheritance for them (v. 8). And he achieves this by a new exodus whereby people from all nations come to God (vv. 9–12). With such good news, no wonder all creation rejoices in verse 13. God has comforted his people and shown compassion on his afflicted.

Sometimes, it's easy to doubt this and become weary. But God assures us he will not forget his people (vv. 15–16) and will multiply his church. Things may seem barren and desolate for a while, and we will go through bereavement. But in time there's a joyous wedding (v. 18), and then a baby boom of unexpected children— too many to provide room for (v. 20), so many we can't work out where they've come from (v. 21). God has accomplished his work, bringing in children from the nations (vv. 22–23), and he will conquer our enemies too (vv. 24–26).

If your group has doubts about identifying Isaiah's servant as Jesus Christ, you might point out that, in addition to the direct New Testament references, the descriptions in Isaiah's servant songs (42:1–9; 49:1–13; 50:4–11; 52:13–53:12) create further connections. Christ's three offices of prophet, priest, and king are present: he is the Prophet whose mouth is like a sharp sword (49:2), the Priest who sprinkles the nations (52:15) and makes intercession (53:12), and the King in whose hand the will of the Lord will prosper (53:10). Additionally, in Isaiah 53 the key moments of the servant's ministry match Christ's earthly and heavenly ministry: his life of rejection, his humble submission and violent death, his burial with the wicked and at the same time with a rich man, his resurrection with a posterity following after him, his ascension to distribute the spoils to many, and his intercession for transgressors. The servant's life foreshadows Christ's life, from his earthly life to his heavenly session and intercession. See, for example, Matthew 26:57–27:61; Philippians 2:6–11; Hebrews 7:25; 1 Peter 2:21–25.

LESSON 8: MAN OF SORROWS

The arm of the Lord in Isaiah 53 is veiled behind the servant's unattractive appearance and the people's rejection of him. The mention of the young plant and the root recalls chapter 11 where Isaiah spoke of a root and shoot from Jesse. But the witnesses did not believe the message about this royal son because, as he entered public life, there was nothing the world found attractive about him. Instead, they despised and rejected him, and hid their faces from him (in Hebrew thought, the face speaks of basic favor, approval, and acceptance). Those who proclaim the servant were first despisers of the servant—something with which every believer can identify. Considering all we did to him, it is remarkable how he took all the griefs and sorrows that burden us in this broken, sin-filled world, and made them his own.

The servant's innocence is seen in the image of a lamb going to the slaughter. He was a sheep who, unlike us, did not wander from the way but instead submitted himself to those who would slaughter him—and in silence, too. Twice we are told that he did not open his mouth, and when he did open it, there was no deceit found in it. Why the emphasis on the mouth? Because mouths reveal hearts, as Isaiah himself had learned in 6:5. Yet under the most intense pressure of oppression and injustice, this servant uttered no angry protests, no words of revenge—no deceit. His silent restraint in the midst of such intense persecution established the basic fact of his innocence. It is clear for all to see—and hear. (You might find it helpful to compare Isaiah's description with Jesus's speech/silence in Matthew 26:57–68; 27:11–14.)

The servant's willingness to suffer is important. Some have called God's punishment of his innocent Son "cosmic child abuse,"[11] and it would be if Jesus had been crushed against his will. But the picture throughout Isaiah 53 is of a willing servant who wants to save his people and emerges from his ordeal victorious, amply rewarded, and still generous—sharing his spoils. For him to pour out his soul unto death for the very ones who rejected him is ultimately not his undoing but his glory and his satisfaction (v. 11), and it is wholly in line with his incomparable love.

LESSON 9: COME TO THE WATERS

Isaiah 55 recognizes that, due to sin and our separation from God, we are restless and dissatisfied beings. Our hearts long for more than this world can offer. And every attempt to be satisfied with something less than God himself falls short of the banquet Isaiah describes. Like eating junk food, it never satisfies but only leaves us hungrier. This banquet picture stands against the popular idea that God is some kind of killjoy. The Bible tells us God is actually a joy giver: In the garden of Eden, he gave *every tree* but one for food—and that one was simply to teach that we are not God, and to offer the opportunity to attain the eternal, permanent joy of obedient fellowship with him. In the promised land, God told his people to go in and enjoy themselves in a land flowing with milk and honey. In Deuteronomy 14:26, God tells them to spend their tithe and feast before him on whatever their appetite craves. People who call God a killjoy have simply not read the Bible.

The blessings of God include satisfactions that simply cannot be found anywhere else: everlasting and absolutely certain covenant love, God-given honor and glory, missionary impact that will be recognized in all the world, and eternal forgiveness of sin from God himself. Even the repentance described in verse 7, though it may feel terrifying and seldom is easy, brings deep joy because of the full and free forgiveness that surely results. You might need to make sure your group understands that repentance is not reaching a certain level of outward obedience (which would never be good enough!) but having an inner change in orientation away from self and toward God. In repentance, we recognize our sins and false satisfactions, are sorry for them, and inwardly turn away from them and toward God instead. This two-part turning, and the fruit that results, is an ongoing process throughout the whole of our life.

LESSON 10: NEW HEAVENS AND NEW EARTH

Remember that we have summarized Isaiah's message as the gospel story of how God saves his people, through judgment, for the transformation of the world. That transformation is where we arrive in chapter 65, and it is marked by joy. The double imperative "be glad and rejoice" covers every possible joyful feeling, and "forever" counters the transience of our earthly joys that come and go. This life will be sustained, permanent, unbreakable, unalloyed joy—coming from the core of our being. And it will be a shared joy with God, who says he will also rejoice in his people.

The passage emphasizes an end to the many futilities and hostilities that characterize our world today, embodied in the futility and hostility brought by death. Death is ruthless, indiscriminate, and untimely—robbing us even if we die at an old age. But God promises that long and certain life awaits us.

Verse 20 is tricky, seeming to suggest that people will still sin and die in the new creation. This would contradict everything the rest of the Bible says about the coming life, so some scholars speculate that this part of Isaiah's prophesy might instead be referring to life in Jerusalem after the exile or to life today as Jesus reigns from heaven. A better interpretation might be to see the references to death and sin as hypothetical: *if* a person were to live a hundred years and then die due to sin's curse (which in our current world would be considered a long life and a blessing), it would be seen as tragic in the world to come. In any case, we need to interpret this relatively unclear part of Scripture in light of passages that are clearer, such as Isaiah 25:6–9, which leaves no doubt that in the new creation death will be swallowed up forever. And the general gist of chapter 65 is still a promise of longevity and certain life.

If verse 25 sounds familiar, realize that it repeats language we saw in chapter 11 (lesson 3).

ENDNOTES

1. I arrived at this big-picture idea by reading Barry Webb, *The Message of Isaiah*, The Bible Speaks Today (Leicester: InterVarsity, 1996), especially 30–33.

2. See J. Alec Motyer, *The Prophecy of Isaiah* (Leicester: InterVarsity, 1993), 124.

3. This thought and several others in the exercise are drawn in part from Thomas Goodwin, *Christ Set Forth and The Heart of Christ in Heaven Towards Sinners on Earth* (Fearn, Scotland: Christian Focus, 2011).

4. Gertrud Schiller, *Iconography of Christian Art* (London: Lund Humphries, 1972), 2:xx.

5. B. Hudson MacLean, *An Introduction to Greek Epigraphy of the Hellenistic and Roman Periods from Alexander the Great Down to the Reign of Constantine* (Ann Arbor, MI: University of Michigan Press, 2002), 208.

6. This comment and others below have been influenced by J. Alec Motyer's moving essay, "Stricken for the Transgression of My People: The Atoning Work of Isaiah's Suffering Servant," in *From Heaven He Came and Sought Her: Definite Atonement in Historical, Biblical, Theological, and Pastoral Perspective*, ed. David Gibson and Jonathan Gibson (Wheaton, IL: Crossway, 2013), 247–66.

7. I'm grateful to Paul Levy for this illustration.

8. C. S. Lewis, *The Lion, the Witch and the Wardrobe* (New York: HarperCollins, 1950), 179, page reference is to the 2002 edition.

9. I am speaking of God here in human terms, known in theological language as anthropopathism (God described in human passions) and anthropomorphism (God described in human form/body parts). God, of course, is an unchangeable spirit—in himself, he cannot be grieved or gladdened. He remains, immutably, in a state of eternal happiness.

10. Motyer, *The Prophecy of Isaiah*, 124.

11. Steve Chalke and Alan Mann, *The Lost Message of Jesus* (Grand Rapids, MI: Zondervan, 2004), 182.

SELECTED BIBLIOGRAPHY

The content of this book is based on a sermon series I preached as a minister at Cambridge Presbyterian Church. My sermon preparation was informed by the following scholars, and their influence at different points is reflected in this book:

Blocher, Henri. *Songs of the Servant*: *Isaiah's Good News*. Vancouver, BC: Regent College Publishing, 2005 [1975].

Motyer, J. Alec. *The Prophecy of Isaiah*. Leicester: InterVarsity, 1993.

Oswalt, John N. *The Book of Isaiah, Chapters 1–39*. NICOT. Grand Rapids, MI: Eerdmans, 1986.

———. *The Book of Isaiah, Chapters 40–66*. NICOT. Grand Rapids, MI: Eerdmans, 1998.

Patston, Kirk. *Isaiah: Surprising Salvation*. Reading the Bible Today. Sydney: Aquila Press, 2010.

Webb, Barry. *The Message of Isaiah*. The Bible Speaks Today. Leicester: InterVarsity, 1996.

My thanks to Jack Klumpenhower for his excellent editorial assistance in preparing this manuscript.

mission
propelled by good news

At Serge we believe that mission begins through the gospel of Jesus Christ bringing God's grace into the lives of believers. This good news also sustains and empowers us to cross nations and cultures to bring the gospel of grace to those whom God is calling to himself.

As a cross-denominational, reformed sending agency with more than two hundred missionaries and twenty-five teams in five continents, we are always looking for people who are ready to take the next step in sharing Christ through:

- **Short-term Teams:** One- to two-week trips oriented around serving overseas ministries while equipping the local church for mission

- **Internships:** Eight-week to nine-month opportunities to learn about missions through serving with our overseas ministry teams

- **Apprenticeships:** Intensive twelve- to twenty-four-month training and ministry opportunities for those discerning their call to cross-cultural ministry

- **Career:** One- to five-year appointments designed to nurture you for a lifetime of ministry

 Grace at the Fray   **Visit us online at: serge.org/mission**

newgrowthpress.com

131

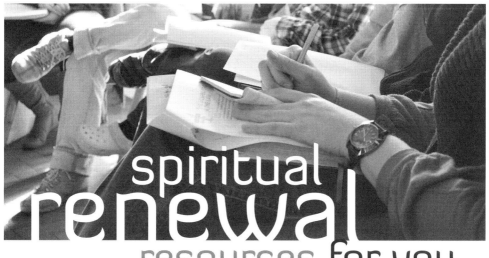

spiritual renewal resources for you

Disciples who are motivated and empowered by grace to reach out to a broken world are handmade, not mass-produced. Serge intentionally grows disciples through curricula, discipleship experiences, and training programs.

Resources for Every Stage of Growth

Serge offers grace-based, gospel-centered studies for every stage of the Christian journey. Every level of our materials focuses on essential aspects of how the Spirit transforms and motivates us through the gospel of Jesus Christ.

- **101**: The Gospel-Centered Series
  Gospel-centered studies on Christian growth, community, work, parenting, and more
- **201**: The Gospel Transformation Series
  These studies go a step deeper into gospel transformation, involve homework and more in-depth Bible study
- **301**: The Sonship Course and Serge Individual Mentoring

Mentored Sonship

For more than twenty-five years Serge has been discipling ministry leaders around the world through our Sonship course to help them experience the freedom and joy of having the gospel transform every part of their lives. A personal discipler will help you apply what you are learning to the daily struggles and situations you face, as well as, model what a gospel-centered faith looks and feels like.

Discipler Training Course

Serge's Discipler Training Course helps you gain biblical understanding and practical wisdom you need to disciple others so they experience substantive, lasting growth in their lives. Available for on-site training or via distance learning, our training programs are ideal for ministry leaders, small group leaders or those seeking to grow in their ability to disciple effectively.

 Grace at the Fray

Find more resources at serge.org

resources and mentoring for every stage of
growth

Every day around the world, Serge teams help people develop and deepen a living, breathing, growing relationship with Jesus. We help people connect with God in ways that are genuinely grace-motivated and increase desire and ability to reach out to others. No matter where you are along the way, we have a series that is right for you.

101: The Gospel-Centered Series

Our *Gospel-Centered* series is simple, deep, and transformative. Each *Gospel-Centered* lesson features an easy-to-read article and provides challenging discussion questions and application questions. Best of all, no outside preparation on the part of the participants is needed! They are perfect for small groups, those who are seeking to develop "gospel DNA" in their organizations and leaders, and contexts where people are still wrestling with what it means to follow Jesus.

201: The Gospel Transformation Series

Our *Gospel Transformation* studies take the themes introduced in our 101-level materials and expand and deepen them. Designed for those seeking to grow through directly studying Scripture, each *Gospel Transformation* lesson helps participants grow in the way they understand and experience God's grace. Ideal for small groups, individuals who are ready for more, and one-on-one mentoring, *Gospel Identity*, *Gospel Growth*, and *Gospel Love* provide substantive material, in easy-to-use, manageable sized studies.

The Sonship Course and Individual Mentoring from Serge

Developed for use with our own missionaries and used for over twenty-five years with thousands of Christian leaders in every corner of the world, *Sonship* sets the standard for whole-person, life transformation through the gospel. Designed to be used with a mentor or in groups ready for a high investment with each other, each lesson focuses on the type of "inductive heart study" that brings about change from the inside out.

 Grace at the Fray

Visit us online at serge.org

newgrowthpress.com